PRENTICE HALL *WRITER'S SOLUTION*

Grammar Practice Book

COPPER

PRENTICE HALL
Upper Saddle River, New Jersey
Needham, Massachusetts

ISBN 0-13-434639-4

1 2 3 4 5 6 7 8 9 10   01 00 99 98 97

PRENTICE HALL
Simon & Schuster Education Group
A VIACOM COMPANY

Contents

VIII Listening and Speaking

1.1 The Noun

A noun is the name of a person, place, or thing.

People	Places	Things
Dr. Linsley	Treasure Island	ship
Jim Hawkins	island	barrel
pirate	mountain	plot
crew	cave	robbery

EXERCISE A: Recognizing Nouns. Underline each noun in the sentences below.

EXAMPLE: Mrs. Nelson has postponed the test until Monday.

1. Several reporters arrived at the scene to interview the survivors.
2. Many young children are afraid of the dark.
3. Our neighbors spent their vacation in the mountains.
4. Jason found his missing sneaker under the couch.
5. Amanda wants to see that movie, too.
6. Without Nancy, our team will surely lose.
7. That tree hasn't lost a single leaf yet.
8. The architect planned for a fountain in the lobby.
9. Phil told only his parents about his fear.
10. Marc cannot see much without his glasses.

EXERCISE B: Adding Nouns to Sentences. Fill in each blank in these sentences with an appropriate noun.

EXAMPLE: ____Alison____ ordered a ___sandwich___ with mustard.

1. The _____ I found had _____ inside.
2. A(n) _____ stopped the _____ at the corner.
3. We asked the _____ to bring us some _____.
4. _____ promised me a(n) _____.
5. The last _____ was a(n) _____.
6. A large _____ grows beside the _____.
7. _____ works at the _____.
8. Some _____ enjoy _____.
9. _____ makes delicious _____.
10. The_____ took a trip to _____.

1.2 Compound Nouns

A compound noun is one noun made by joining two or more words. Compound nouns are written in three different ways: as single words, as hyphenated words, and as separate words.

COMPOUND NOUNS		
Single Words	**Hyphenated Words**	**Separate Words**
plaything	jack-in-the-box	teddy bear
grandmother	baby-sitter	day care
classmate	teen-ager	high school

EXERCISE A: Recognizing Compound Nouns. Circle each compound noun in the sentences below.

EXAMPLE: Mom made some (hard sauce) to serve with the (gingerbread.)

1. Morning-glories climb up the lamppost.
2. That paperback became a best seller almost immediately.
3. After a number of successful dramatic plays, the playwright is now working on a musical comedy.
4. Kevin Parker is studying political science.
5. A passer-by must have found my wallet on the sidewalk.
6. The reporter rushed to get the story to the city desk before deadline.
7. Paul had his bathing suit and towel in his backpack.
8. The caretaker has a skeleton key that opens all the doors.
9. Do not unfasten your seat belt until the airplane has come to a complete stop at the gate.
10. I had trouble using chopsticks to eat my chow mein.

EXERCISE B: More Work with Compound Nouns. Follow the directions for Exercise A, above.

1. My grandfather recites nursery rhymes to my little cousin.
2. How do you write seventy-seven in Roman numerals?
3. My brother's roommate was first runner-up in the contest.
4. The footnote contained a cross-reference to another book.
5. My cousin lost a contact lens on the shag rug in the bedroom.
6. The folk singer has recorded a song based on the hero of a tall tale.
7. The stage manager will supervise the final run-through of the play.
8. The follow-up showed that the treatment had lowered the patient's blood pressure.
9. Kneepads are good safety devices for people who use skateboards.
10. A bookkeeper must have legible handwriting.

1.3 Common and Proper Nouns

A common noun names any one of a group of people, places, or things. A proper noun names a specific person, place, or thing. The important words in proper nouns are always capitalized.

Common Nouns		Proper Nouns	
planet	language	Uranus	Russian
street	day	Market Place	New Year's Day
horse	train	Flicka	the *Silver Meteor*
woman	story	Mrs. Bailey	"A Day's Wait"

EXERCISE A: Recognizing Proper Nouns. Write the proper noun in each sentence on the line after the sentence. Use capital letters correctly.

EXAMPLE: Our former neighbors now live on maple street. __*Maple Street*__

1. Fireworks are traditional on the fourth of july. _____

2. The new principal is mrs. jacobson. _____

3. Every year my aunt takes her children to see santa claus. _____

4. We play our last game against the lancers. _____

5. The beach boys will perform at the festival. _____

6. We have a family reunion every august. _____

7. That poem was written by henry wadsworth longfellow. _____

8. The box on the hall table came from uncle albert. _____

9. That best seller has just been translated into japanese. _____

10. Did you take the stairs to the top of the washington monument? _____

EXERCISE B: Distinguishing Between Common and Proper Nouns. Write each noun from the box in the proper column. Write a related noun in the other column to complete the chart. The first two are done to show you how.

1. book		4. capital		7. Sitting Bull		10. South America	
2. Broadway		5. comic strip		8. Eleanor Roosevelt		11. Statue of Liberty	
3. building		6. Yankee Stadium		9. school		12. teacher	

COMMON NOUNS

1. *book* _____

2. *street* _____

3. _____

4. _____

5. _____

6. _____

7. _____

8. _____

9. _____

10. _____

11. _____

12. _____

PROPER NOUNS

The Time Machine

Broadway

_____

_____

_____

_____

_____

_____

_____

_____

_____

_____

2.1 The Pronoun

A pronoun takes the place of a noun. The noun that is replaced by a pronoun is called the antecedent.

PRONOUNS AND ANTECEDENTS
Person   The *forecaster* revised *her* weather forecast.
Place   When we got to the *amusement park*, we found that *it* was closed.
Thing   All those *umbrellas* have holes in *them*.

EXERCISE A: Recognizing Pronouns and Antecedents. Circle the pronoun in each sentence below. Underline its antecedent.

EXAMPLE: The <u>campers</u> had a variety of foods in (their) backpacks.

1. Alison forgot to give her mother the telephone message.
2. Someone let the parakeets out of their cage.
3. Iowa is famous for its corn and beef.
4. Several students forgot their homework assignments.
5. Mr. Wilson will retire next year. He has worked at First Bank for forty years.
6. Whenever Angie visits, she wants to play Trivial Pursuit.
7. The members of the committee will reveal their plans next week.
8. Mom is visiting Uncle Bert in Oklahoma. Dad will join her next week.
9. The Mississippi River has its origin at Lake Itaska in Minnesota.
10. Some identical twins enjoy fooling their friends and acquaintances.

EXERCISE B: Using Pronouns in Sentences. Write an appropriate pronoun in each blank to complete the sentence.

EXAMPLE: The Haywards are spending the weekend at ___their___ cabin at Loon Lake.

1. Did David bring _____ camera along?
2. Chipmunks make _____ homes in underground tunnels.
3. The children rebelled because _____ summer schedules were too busy.
4. Luke complained of pains in _____ ankle.
5. The lion had a thorn in _____ paw.
6. The house will look better when _____ has a fresh coat of paint.
7. Rachel has kept every story _____ has written since first grade.
8. The neighbors complained that _____ couldn't sleep because of the noise.
9. The O'Shaughnesseys showed slides of _____ trip to Ireland.
10. The sauce has just a hint of garlic in _____ .

2.2 Personal Pronouns

Personal pronouns refer to (1) the person speaking or writing, (2) the person listening or reading, or (3) the topic (person, place, or thing) being discussed or written about.

PERSONAL PRONOUNS		
	Singular	**Plural**
First Person **Second Person** **Third Person**	I, me, my, mine you, your, yours he, him, his she, her, hers it, its	we, us, our, ours you, your, yours they, them, their, theirs

EXERCISE A: Recognizing Personal Pronouns. Underline the personal pronoun in each sentence. On the lines after each sentence write *1st, 2nd,* or *3rd* to tell the person and *S* or *P* to tell whether it is singular or plural.

EXAMPLE: Pete and Aaron have their parents' permission to go. __*3rd*__ __*P*__

1. Class, open your test booklets. _____ _____

2. Last summer I took tennis lessons. _____ _____

3. The house with the pale blue shutters is ours. _____ _____

4. Dana was surprised that she won first prize. _____ _____

5. Have you finished with the paper, Frank? _____ _____

6. Both Phil and Steve lost their library cards. _____ _____

7. The kitten has black markings around its eyes. _____ _____

8. Dad has scheduled his vacation for the last week in July. _____ _____

9. Please tell us how to get to Jefferson Park. _____ _____

10. That orange sweatshirt is mine. _____ _____

EXERCISE B: Adding Personal Pronouns to Sentences. Fill in the blank with an appropriate personal pronoun to complete each sentence.

EXAMPLE: Did you remember to bring your lunch with __*you*__?

1. Both Tim and I enjoyed _____ trip to the United Nations.

2. The Barkers are moving into _____ new house next week.

3. I wish someone would explain that magic trick to _____ .

4. Louisa wrote in _____ diary every night.

5. Did you and Ben bring _____ swimming trunks?

6. Mr. Sawyer told us where to find the key to _____ desk.

7. That company gives _____ employees excellent benefits.

8. Justin was sorry that _____ had been so rude.

9. Mrs. Hawkins is very popular with all of _____ students.

10. We arrived at the game after _____ had started.

2.3 Demonstrative Pronouns

A demonstrative pronoun points out a person, place, or thing.

DEMONSTRATIVE PRONOUNS		
	Singular	**Plural**
Nearby	this	these
Farther	that	those

EXERCISE A: Recognizing Demonstrative Pronouns. Underline the demonstrative pronoun in each sentence. Circle the noun it refers to.

EXAMPLE: This must be the (book) you ordered.

1. That was a loud firecracker.
2. All the pastries look good, but I think I'll try one of these.
3. These are tomatoes from our garden.
4. Isn't this the sweater I lent you?
5. Those were the best meatballs I ever had.
6. That is the woman I was telling you about.
7. These are the curtains my grandmother made.
8. Doesn't this stew smell good?
9. That was a terrific movie we saw last night.
10. The best pictures I have ever taken are those of my baby cousin.

EXERCISE B: Using Demonstrative Pronouns in Sentences. Fill in each blank with an appropriate demonstrative pronoun to complete the sentence.

EXAMPLE: Those slacks are a great color, but ___these___ are more practical.

1. _____ is the first eclipse I have ever seen.
2. _____ was a thrilling experience.
3. The tomatoes on the windowsill are ripe, but _____ on the vines are still green.
4. Bob refused to believe the warnings, and _____ was his first mistake.
5. All of Mrs. Parker's meals are good, but _____ is outstanding.
6. Of all his paintings, _____ that he did in his youth are the most realistic.
7. That fabric looks good on the couch, but _____ is a better color.
8. If you think these roses are beautiful, you should see _____ in the back yard!
9. Miss Walters said that of all my essays _____ is the best one.
10. Those cookies on the trays are still hot, but _____ on the plate are ready to eat.

3.1 The Verb

A verb expresses the action or condition of a person, place, or thing.

VERBS	
Action	**Condition**
amuse	was
inspected	seems
remember	become
begins	am
discovered	appear

EXERCISE A: Recognizing Verbs. Underline the verb in each sentence. On the line at the right, tell whether the verb expresses action or condition.

EXAMPLE: Marlene <u>memorized</u> her speech in half an hour. ___*action*___

1. Judd offered a reward for the lost wallet. _____

2. This stew tastes too salty. _____

3. Shannon always wears funny hats. _____

4. At the age of five, Larry gave his first recital. _____

5. Even after the argument, Gary remained loyal to his old friend. _____

6. We felt refreshed after a shower and a cold drink. _____

7. Linda played shortstop during the last half of the season. _____

8. That pitcher is famous for his curve ball. _____

9. Laura seems upset about something. _____

10. We carefully planned every detail of the party. _____

EXERCISE B: Adding Verbs to Sentences. Complete each sentence by filling in the blank with a verb of the kind called for in parentheses.

EXAMPLE: Lauren ___*practices*___ the piano two hours every day. (action)

1. Marc _____ soccer better than basketball. (action)

2. The nurse _____ the patient's temperature. (action)

3. We _____ disappointed in the outcome of the game. (condition)

4. Paula _____ good in that shade of blue. (condition)

5. Kevin _____ the experiment several times. (action)

6. The child's endless questions _____ her parents. (action)

7. Yesterday a record number of fans _____ the game. (action)

8. Those leaves _____ orange in autumn. (condition)

9. That song _____ better on the piano than on the guitar. (condition)

10. Gerry _____ her lesson the hard way. (action)

3.2 Action Verbs

An action verb indicates the action of a person or thing. The action can be visible or mental.

ACTION VERBS	
Visible Actions	**Mental Actions**
blow	wonder
follow	forget
run	annoy
write	pretend
stir	consider

EXERCISE A: Identifying Action Verbs. Underline the verb in each sentence below.

EXAMPLE: The bloodhound lost the scent at the edge of the creek.

1. The teacher explained the directions again.
2. We planted four kinds of lettuce in our garden.
3. Lana teased her brother about his socks.
4. Steve borrowed lunch money from me again today.
5. Despite a number of fielding errors, the home team won.
6. Grandma promised all of us rewards for our report cards.
7. Dad estimated the distance fairly accurately.
8. Sherman's army left a trail of destruction behind it.
9. The auctioneer started the bidding at fifty dollars.
10. At least three students failed the math test.

EXERCISE B: Adding Action Verbs to Sentences. Complete each sentence by filling in the blank with an action verb of the kind indicated in parentheses.

EXAMPLE: The committee __considered__ the choices carefully.   (mental)

1. Too late, Julie _____ the right answer.   (mental)
2. Anthony _____ butter on his potato.   (mental)
3. Waiting for news, Dennis _____ back and forth in the hallway.   (visible)
4. That puzzle _____ everyone.   (mental)
5. The prince and princess _____ hands with everyone at the party.   (visible)
6. We _____ everywhere for Mom's missing keys.   (visible)
7. Mr. Salvin _____ his students to work hard.   (mental)
8. Phil _____ the ball down the court.   (visible)
9. The announcer _____ the winning ticket from the barrel.   (visible)
10. Marci _____ her ticket to the flight attendant.   (visible)

3.3 | Linking Verbs

A linking verb joins a noun or pronoun at or near the beginning of a sentence with a word at or near the end. The word at the end identifies or describes the noun or pronoun.

LINKING VERBS		
Forms of *Be*		**Other Linking Verbs**

am	am being	can be	have been	appear	seem
are	are being	could be	has been	become	smell
is	is being	may be	had been	feel	sound
was	was being	might be	could have been	grow	stay
were	were being	must be	may have been	look	taste
		shall be	might have been	remain	turn
		should be	must have been		
		will be	shall have been		
		would be	should have been		
			will have been		
			would have been		

EXERCISE A: Recognizing Linking Verbs. Circle the linking verb in each sentence. Then underline the words that are linked by the verb.

EXAMPLE: Penny grew tall over the summer.

1. Beginning violinists usually sound terrible for the first few weeks.
2. Rail service in this area has been irregular recently.
3. With Steven away on vacation, I am bored.
4. The crowd became restless because of the long delay.
5. Many of Erica's classmates were jealous of her success.
6. Jerry feels listless much of the time recently.
7. Louisa should have been more careful about her facts.
8. Those cookies smell delicious.
9. Linus feels secure with his blanket.
10. Alicia remained calm throughout the blackout.

EXERCISE B: Adding Linking Verbs to Sentences. Complete each sentence by writing an appropriate linking verb in the blank. Then underline the two words that are linked by the verb.

EXAMPLE: Jason ___appeared___ nervous at the beginning of his speech.

1. Nancy _____ lucky at winning the drawing.
2. Some of the questions _____ hard to understand.
3. The order _____ too large for one shipment.
4. Dorothy _____ surprised to be back in Kansas.
5. The store _____ open even after the fire.
6. Phil _____ confused about the announcement.
7. The weather _____ cold during the night.
8. Luke _____ an actor in spite of his parents' objections.
9 Jennie _____ excited about her news.
10. M-m-m-m, something _____ good in here.

3.4 | Helping Verbs

A helping verb is a verb that comes before the main verb and adds to its meaning.

COMMON HELPING VERBS			
am	being	could	must
are	been	do	shall
is	have	does	should
was	has	did	will
were	had	may	would
be	can	might	

EXERCISE A: Identifying Helping Verbs. Underline each helping verb in the sentences below. Circle the main verb in each verb pharase.

EXAMPLE: Carol has been (studying) French this summer.

1. The kitchen staff will be serving from 4:30 until 9:00.
2. The train should arrive any minute.
3. Dr. Young has examined our dog.
4. My little brother can be a real pest sometimes.
5. The secretary has ordered a new supply of erasers.
6. Perhaps Jake really did forget his boots.
7. Grandma may know the answer.
8. Judson has taken a job at the supermarket.
9. I am waiting for a phone call.
10. Elsa should have tried harder.

EXERCISE B: Adding Helping Verbs to Sentences. Fill in each blank with an appropriate helping verb.

EXAMPLE: Paul __is__ taking a computer course at summer school.

1. Surely everyone _____ be surprised to see us.
2. Someone _____ _____ told Mandy about the surprise party.
3. Uncle Dave _____ _____ working at the bank for twenty years.
4. Susan _____ _____ visiting her grandparents.
5. I _____ seen that movie twice already.
6. The run of the play _____ _____ extended for two more weeks.
7. Lou _____ need some help.
8. Patty _____ be sorry she said that.
9. I _____ _____ studied harder for that test.
10. Quentin _____ _____ painting the house all summer.

4.1 The Adjective

An adjective is a word that describes something.

QUESTIONS ANSWERED BY ADJECTIVES	
What Kind?	A *huge* monster, *ugly* and *hairy*, arose from the sea.
	She is *talented* and *hard-working*.
Which One?	*That* bike belongs to me. I need *those* nails.
How Many? How Much?	*Few* tickets remain. *Some* cake is left.

EXERCISE A: Identifying Adjectives. Underline the adjectives in the sentences below.

EXAMPLE: <u>Tired</u> and <u>hungry</u>, the campers found the camp a <u>welcome</u> sight.

1. That popular star has many enthusiastic and loyal fans.
2. The smallest building on that vast estate will be a guest house.
3. The two old maple trees are beautiful in the fall.
4. That large white house looks expensive.
5. Nervous and excited, I went up to accept the blue ribbon.
6. Only an expert fisherman could have caught an enormous fish like that one.
7. As the withered old woman approached the microphone, the audience became silent.
8. Fat shoelaces in neon colors were a brief but colorful fad.
9. Diligent and determined, Len soon became expert at tennis.
10. That feathery green fern looks beautiful in the front window.

EXERCISE B: Adding Adjectives to Sentences. Fill in each blank with an appropriate adjective. Circle the word it describes.

EXAMPLE: (Jenny) appeared ___*angry*___ about something.

1. Janice has a(n) _____ appetite for someone her size.
2. A(n) _____ snake crawled out from under a rock.
3. The view from the top of the mountain was _____ .
4. Tanya seemed _____ for our friendship.
5. One _____ student stood off to one side watching the others.
6. The team, _____ and _____ , left the field amid cheers.
7. Check carefully before riding your bike into _____ traffic.
8. The farmers hoped for a(n) _____ harvest.
9. The police gave Tom a citation for his _____ rescue.
10. The _____ fish swam back and forth in the _____ tank.

4.2 Articles

The is the definite article. It points to a specific person, place, or thing. *A* and *an* are the indefinite articles. They point to any member of a group of similar people, places, or things.

ARTICLES		
Definite Article	Indefinite Article Before Consonant Sounds	Indefinite Article Before Vowel Sounds
the woman	a young woman	an old woman
the underbrush	a unique gift	an ugly episode
the operator	a one-sided argument	an only child

EXERCISE A: Identifying Articles. Underline the articles in the sentences below. Above each one, write *D* if it is a definite article or *I* if it is indefinite.

EXAMPLE: <u>A</u> robin built its nest in <u>the</u> tree outside my window.

1. Sharon is taking a writing course at summer school.
2. Alison has a book on reserve at the library.
3. Everyone at the party wore an unusual hat.
4. The coach has called an extra practice before the game on Saturday.
5. We had a good time on the camping trip.
6. The sentence on the second line needs a period at the end.
7. The child drew a picture of a visitor from another planet.
8. An unfortunate incident broke up the party early.
9. The principal made an announcement about the class trip.
10. We all made an effort to be polite to the newcomers.

EXERCISE B: Using Indefinite Articles. Fill in each blank with the correct indefinite article.

EXAMPLE: __*an*__ unsuccessful attempt

1. _____ unified paragraph
2. _____ exciting opportunity
3. _____ outstanding student
4. _____ colorful garden
5. _____ friendly discussion

6. _____ elegant restaurant
7. _____ willing worker
8. _____ perfect day
9. _____ playful cat
10. _____ early riser

4.3 | Proper Adjectives

A proper adjective is (1) a proper noun used as an adjective or (2) an adjective formed from a proper noun.

PROPER ADJECTIVES	
Proper Nouns Used as Adjectives	**Proper Adjective Forms**
Philadelphia lawyer *Franklin* stove *United States Army* base	*Parisian* restaurant *Jeffersonian* democracy *American* citizen

EXERCISE A: Identifying Proper Adjectives. Underline the proper adjective in each sentence. Then circle the noun it modifies.

EXAMPLE: My (uncle) is Chinese.

1. Scandinavian winters are long and cold.
2. We went down the river in an Eskimo kayak.
3. The class had a perfect June day for graduation.
4. Chinese restaurants are becoming very popular.
5. The cruise will stop at several Caribbean ports.
6. Do you like Charlie Chaplin films?
7. The coffee was made from fresh-ground Brazilian coffee beans.
8. Italian ice is a refreshing summertime dessert.
9. I am reading a collection of Greek myths.
10. Mom has always admired that Monet painting.

EXERCISE B: Using Proper Adjectives to Modify Nouns. Rewrite each group of words to include a proper adjective before the underlined noun.

EXAMPLE: a vacation in Europe ____*a European vacation*____

1. a new video made by Michael Jackson _____
2. the soccer team from Australia _____
3. an opera written by an Italian _____
4. a diplomat from the Middle East _____
5. an island in the Mediterranean _____
6. the overture by Tchaikovsky _____
7. a spokesman in the White House _____
8. snowstorms in Alaska _____
9. the potato from Idaho _____
10. a representative from California _____

4.4 Possessive Adjectives

A personal pronoun can be used as an adjective if it modifies a noun.

PERSONAL PRONOUNS USED AS POSSESSIVE ADJECTIVES	
Singular	**Plural**
I lost *my* sneakers.	He and I have had *our* differences.
You will need *your* boots, Ed.	Students, you may take out *your* books.
Alana enjoyed *her* trip.	
Ben lent me *his* notes.	Many students ride *their* bikes to school.
The paper changed *its* format.	

EXERCISE A: Recognizing Possessive Adjectives. Underline the pronoun used as an adjective in each sentence. Underline its antecedent twice, and circle the noun it modifies.

EXAMPLE: Andrew has chosen a biography for his (book report.)

1. The orchestra played the *1812 Overture* for its finale.
2. Mandy went to Chicago with her family over spring break.
3. The record became a hit during its first week on the racks.
4. The stars have donated their services for the charity concert.
5. Gina, you should have proofread your work more carefully.
6. I wish I had brought my umbrella.
7. Rick brought his guitar to the party.
8. Betsy and I have always shared all our secrets with each other.
9. Many people brought their folding chairs to the fireworks.
10. Denise and Len are visiting their grandparents this weekend.

EXERCISE B: Using Possessive Adjectives in Sentences. Write an appropriate possessive pronoun in each blank. Underline the noun it modifies.

EXAMPLE: Len and I enjoyed ___our___ trip to the museum.

1. Tim and Janet have been using _____ computer for school work.
2. Mark carefully put _____ coin collection away.
3. Mom is famous all over town for _____ lemon meringue pie.
4. That magazine has doubled _____ circulation in two years.
5. Thomas Jefferson designed _____ own home at Monticello.
6. I cannot take very good pictures with _____ camera.
7. The network revised _____ program schedule because of the news conference.
8. Lily writes to _____ family every day while she is at camp.
9. Ramon takes _____ new puppy everywhere with him.
10. Have you started writing _____ report yet?

5.1 The Adverb

An adverb is a word that modifies a verb, an adjective, or another adverb.

WHAT ADVERBS TELL ABOUT VERBS	
Where?	Put the packges *there*.
	We held the party *outside*.
When?	I will meet you *later*.
	Grandma is coming *today*.
In What Way?	The elephant moved *awkwardly*.
	The shortstop runs *fast*.
To What Extent?	Janet was *completely* honest.
	Lucy seems *very* upset

EXERCISE A: Identifying Adverbs. Underline the adverb in each sentence below. On the line after the sentence, write the question the adverb answers.

EXAMPLE: The teacher <u>carefully</u> explained the experiment. __*In what way?*__

1. My best friend's family has moved away. _____

2. Jason was thoroughly disgusted by the display. _____

3 Tony always finishes all his work on time. _____

4. Roses will grow well in that location. _____

5. Kevin seemed unusually excited at the party. _____

6. Grandpa is shy about telling people about his adventures at sea. _____

7. Martha will be here by dinnertime. _____

8. Phil worked hard on his science project. _____

9. Mr. Murphy is a truly dedicated teacher. _____

10. My father can take us home after the movie. _____

EXERCISE B: More Work with Adverbs. Underline the adverb(s) in each sentence. Then circle the word each adverb modifies.

EXAMPLE: Jeff was <u>very</u> (unhappy) about his lost puppy.

1. That new baby seldom cries.
2. Yesterday I discovered a leak in the boat.
3. Our mail usually arrives in the afternoon.
4. Gary did extremely well at his first recital.
5. Lenore is sometimes careless.
6. We gradually solved the puzzle.
7. The club has two large parties annually.
8. The neighbors were quite annoyed by the loud noise.
9. The ice melted rapidly in the sun.
10. Paul practices his scales diligently.

5.2 Adverb or Adjective?

If a noun or pronoun is modified by a word, that word is an adjective. If a verb, adjective, or adverb is modified by a word, that word is an adverb.

DISTINGUISHING BETWEEN ADJECTIVES AND ADVERBS	
Adjectives	**Adverbs**
We'd better have a *closer* look.	Ed moved *closer* to the stage.
That is a *weekly* magazine.	The club meets *weekly*.
That was a *hard* job.	She works *hard* for her money.

EXERCISE A: Distinguishing Between Adjectives and Adverbs. Write whether the underlined word in each sentence is an adjective or an adverb.

EXAMPLE: Turn <u>left</u> at the first intersection. ___*adverb*___

1. I have never seen a <u>faster</u> horse than that one. _____

2. The nurse should have acted <u>faster</u>. _____

3. Joe made a sharp <u>left</u> turn just past the bridge. _____

4. The old man's stories always seem <u>endless</u>. _____

5. Marcia made a <u>sudden</u> move toward the water. _____

6. Wendy may have taken a <u>later</u> train. _____

7. The mother hummed <u>quietly</u> to the infant in her arms. _____

8. Do you think the watermelon is <u>cold</u> yet? _____

9. Harvey watched the parade go <u>past</u>. _____

10. The plane departed <u>later</u> than scheduled. _____

EXERCISE B: Writing Adjectives and Adverbs in Sentences. Write two sentences for each of the words in parentheses. In the first sentence, use the word as an adjective; in the second, use it as an adverb.

EXAMPLE: (harder) ___*That test was harder than I thought it would be.*___
___*Grace worked harder than ever on her math.*___

1. (upside-down) _____

_____

2. (backward) _____

_____

3. (early) _____

_____

4. (high) _____

_____

5. (only) _____

_____

6.1 The Preposition

A preposition relates a noun or pronoun to another word in the sentence.

PREPOSITIONS		
We ordered pizza	with besides instead of	meatballs.

EXERCISE A: Identifying Prepositions. Circle the preposition(s) in each sentence below. The number in parentheses tells how many to look for.

EXAMPLE: Gerry left (without) a word (to) anyone.   (2)

1. A new family has moved into the house next to ours.   (2)
2. The club isn't much fun without Sharon.   (1)
3. Among the three of us, we had just enough money for a pizza.   (3)
4. Because of that incident, the families do not speak to each other.   (2)
5. We watched the fireworks display from a spot across the river.   (2)
6. Draw a line through any words that are not needed.   (1)
7. The rake has been leaning against the garage since yesterday.   (2)
8. A letter for Mike is on the table in the hall.   (3)
9. You will be safe from the mosquitoes until dusk.   (2)
10. No one except Judy's mother baked brownies.   (1)

EXERCISE B: Using Prepositions in Sentences. Fill in each blank with a preposition to complete the sentences below.

EXAMPLE: We agreed to meet __*before*__ dinner.

1. Carl has ridden his bike _____ the river.
2. I haven't seen Louise _____ a month.
3. We waited _____ six o'clock for the train to arrive.
4. A crowd of people pressed _____ the movie star.
5. I found my sneakers _____ the couch.
6. Many people became restless _____ the long delay.
7. I am reading a book _____ Judy Blume.
8. Basketball is my favorite sport _____ baseball.
9. The realtor took us _____ a number of houses.
10. Fred sits _____ me in math class.

6.2 Preposition or Adverb?

A preposition will always be part of a prepositional phrase. An adverb can stand alone.

DISTINGUISHING BETWEEN PREPOSITIONS AND ADVERBS	
Prepositions	**Adverbs**
We walked *along* the river.	We took the dog *along*.
A car raced *up* the street.	Everyone stood *up*.
I will be there *before* seven.	I have never seen her *before*.

EXERCISE A: Distinguishing Between Prepositions and Adverbs. Write whether the underlined word in each sentence is a preposition or an adverb.

EXAMPLE: Sign your name on the line below. ___*adverb*___

1. We watched the clouds float by. _____

2. Turn left just beyond the apple orchard. _____

3. Did you bring the paper in? _____

4. A large crowd gathered outside the ticket office. _____

5. The skis are in the garage behind the sleds. _____

6. These belong in the cupboard below the kitchen sink. _____

7. The concert was planned by the performers themselves. _____

8. Remember to leave your rubbers outside. _____

9. Did you see the headline in tonight's paper? _____

10. We seem to have left Robbie behind. _____

EXERCISE B: Writing Prepositions and Adverbs in Sentences. Write two sentences for each word given in parentheses. In the first sentence, use the word as a preposition; in the second, use it as an adverb.

EXAMPLE: (besides) ___*Besides Alice, we should invite Mark and Kathy.*___
___*We are very tired, and we are hungry besides.*___

1. (above) _____

_____

2. (inside) _____

_____

3. (off) _____

_____

4. (near) _____

_____

5. (underneath) _____

_____

7.1 The Conjunction

Conjunctions connect words, groups of words, and whole sentences.

USING COORDINATING CONJUNCTIONS	
Nouns	The stew needs more *onions* and *carrots*.
Pronouns	Give the message to *him* or *me*.
Verbs	He *would* not *eat* nor *sleep*.
Adjectives	The runner was *exhausted* but *victorious*.
Adverbs	Mark spoke *clearly* and *forcefully*.
Prepositional Phrases	The gardner works *with great care* yet *without pleasure*.
Sentences	*We held our breath,* for *the figure moved closer.*
	Sandy missed the bus, so *we took her home.*

EXERCISE A: Recognizing Coordinating Conjunctions. Circle the coordinating conjunction in each sentence. Underline the words or word groups it joins.

EXAMPLE: Throughout the stormy night (and) into the morning, rescuers searched the cove.

1. Should I use green or blue for the lettering?
2. The pianist performed with great accuracy but without much feeling.
3. Carol and Luke are finalists in the spelling bee.
4. We arrived early, so we could get good seats for the concert.
5. Jason or Madeline should be able to give you directions.
6. The crowd was somewhat noisy yet otherwise well-behaved.
7. The puppy would not sit nor stay before it went to obedience school.
8. We took the subway to the ballpark, for we knew traffic would be heavy.
9. The children worked busily but quietly on their projects.
10. A combination of luck and skill is needed to win that game.

EXERCISE B: Writing Sentences with Coordinating Conjunctions. Follow the directions for each numbered item to write a sentence of your own.

EXAMPLE: Use *for* to join two sentences.
        High waves tossed the small boat, for a storm had come up unexpectedly.

1. Use *and* to join two prepositional phrases.

   _____

2. Use *but* to join two adjectives.

   _____

3. Use *so* to join two sentences.

   _____

4. Use *yet* to join two adverbs.

   _____

5. Use *or* to join two pronouns.

   _____

7.2 Correlative Conjunctions

Correlative conjunctions are pairs of conjunctions that connect words or word groups.

USING CORRELATIVE CONJUNCTIONS	
Words Joined	**Examples**
Nouns	At the party, Jen served both *hamburgers* and *hot dogs*.
Pronouns	Mom wants to know whether *you* or *I* will set the table.
Verbs	Danny not only *entered* but also *won* the marathon.
Adjectives	The house was neither *attractive* nor *affordable*.
Adverbs	He spoke both *rapidly* and *clearly*.
Prepositional Phrases	You will find the books you need either *on reserve* or *in the reference room*.
Sentences	Not only *did* we bake the pies, but *we also* sold them.

EXERCISE A: Finding Correlative Conjunctions. Circle both parts of the correlative conjunction in each sentence and underline the words or word groups it connects.

EXAMPLE: I wonder (whether) it will <u>rain</u> (or) <u>snow</u> during the night.

1. Ellen usually either walks or rides her bike to school.
2. This pie crust is not only tender but also flaky.
3. Both Paul and his family are Tiger fans.
4. My new record was neither in its jacket nor on the turntable.
5. Do you know whether Shana or her sister took the message?
6. The dinner includes either salad or a vegetable.
7. Ben not only set the table but also washed the dishes.
8. Either Fran will make the arrangements, or Mom will be angry.
9. My sneakers are neither in the closet nor under my bed.
10. I like both sausage and peppers in my sandwich.

EXERCISE B: Writing Sentences with Correlative Conjunctions. Follow the directions for each numbered item to write sentences of your own.

EXAMPLE: Use *either . . . or* to join two adjectives.
      Only someone who is either brave or crazy would take that job.

1. Use *neither . . . nor* to join two adverbs.

   _____

2. Use *whether . . . or* to join two pronouns.

   _____

3. Use *either . . . or* to join two sentences.

   _____

4. Use *not only . . . but also* to join two prepositional phrases.

   _____

5. Use *both . . . and* to join two verbs.

   _____

8.1 The Interjection

Interjections are words that express sudden excitement or strong feeling.

SOME INTERJECTIONS				
ah	fine	huh	oops	ugh
aha	golly	hurray	ouch	well
alas	gosh	my	psst	whew
boy	great	nonsense	sh	wonderful
darn	hey	oh	terrific	wow

EXERCISE A: Recognizing Interjections. Underline the interjection in each sentence.

EXAMPLE: <u>Brother</u>! It surely is hot in here.

1. Nonsense! Who would ever believe a story like that?
2. Gosh, I wish I had thought of that.
3. Terrific! What a great hit that was!
4. Ugh! What is that awful smell?
5. Sh, the baby is sleeping.
6. Oh, no! What a mess I made!
7. Whew, that was a close call.
8. Alas, I should have studied harder.
9. My, what an unkind thing that was to say!
10. Psst, listen to this.

EXERCISE B: Writing Interjections in Sentences. Fill in each blank with an appropriate interjection to complete the sentence.

EXAMPLE: ____*Hush*____, don't say anything now.

1. _____! How spectacular the fireworks were!
2. _____, that was a silly thing to say.
3. _____! I just banged my thumb.
4. _____, that jar slipped out of my hand.
5. _____! Danny wouldn't say such a thing!
6. _____! That was a wonderful movie.
7. _____! This is the book I have been looking for.
8. _____, wait for me!
9. _____! We won!
10. _____? I never heard that version before.

9.1 Identifying Parts of Speech

The eight parts of speech all do different kinds of work within sentences.

THE EIGHT PARTS OF SPEECH		
Parts of Speech	What They Do in a Sentence	Examples
Noun	Names a person, place, or thing	The boy has a red truck.
Pronoun	Takes the place of a noun	He plays with it.
Verb	Expresses an action or condition	Dad trucks fruit long distances. The boy seems happy.
Adjective	Modifies a noun or pronoun	His business is successful.
Adverb	Modifies a verb, an adjective, or another adverb	Tim spelled the word correctly.
Preposition	Relates a noun or pronoun to another word	Put your pencil on your desk.
Conjunction	Connects words, groups of words, or sentences	Pete or Judy will bring the soda, and then we'll be all set.
Interjection	Shows sudden excitement or strong feeling	Ouch! I just stuck my finger.

EXERCISE A: Identifying Parts of Speech. On the blank after each sentence, write the part of speech of the underlined word.

EXAMPLE: You should play underline outside on such a pretty day. ___adverb___

1. The outside of the house needs lots of work. _____

2. We left the package outside the front door. _____

3. The outfielder made a spectacular catch. _____

4. Unfortunately, we didn't catch anything on our fishing trip. _____

5. My, that was a foolish thing to do. _____

6. A small boy found my wallet in the park. _____

7. Grandma has just made chocolate-chip cookies. _____

8. The judge passed a just sentence. _____

9. No one but Jennifer knows our plans. _____

10. The team played well, but they still lost. _____

EXERCISE B: Using Words as Different Parts of Speech. Write two sentences for each word given in parentheses. Use the word as a different part of speech in each sentence.

EXAMPLE: (type) ___What type of bike were you looking for?___
___I cannot type very quickly.___

1. (well) _____

_____

2. (down) _____

_____

3. (call) _____

_____

4. (around) _____

_____

5. (mine) _____

_____

10.1 The Two Parts of a Sentence

Every complete sentence contains a subject and a predicate. The subject tells who or what the sentence is about. The predicate tells something about the subject. The simple subject is a noun or pronoun that answers the question *Who?* or *What?* about the sentence. The simple predicate is the verb that expresses the action done by or to the subject or tells what the condition of the subject is. In the chart below, simple subjects are underlined once and simple predicates are underlined twice.

SIMPLE SUBJECTS AND SIMPLE PREDICATES
The <u>owner</u> of the hat never <u>returned</u>.
These <u>flowers</u> <u>bloom</u> late in the fall.
<u>Several</u> of the new inventions <u>were</u> very clever.

EXERCISE A: Finding Simple Subjects and Simple Predicates. Underline the simple subject once and the simple predicate twice in each sentence below.

EXAMPLE: The <u>rain</u> <u>stopped</u> in the afternoon.

1. A beachball rolled onto the baseball diamond.
2. Dachshunds were bred to hunt badgers.
3. A book about vampires was missing.
4. Several people reported the accident.
5. Len speaks with a slight Australian accent.
6. The sink was full of dirty dishes.
7. Inspector Low held the paper up to the light.
8. Mr. Bixby rarely assigns homework.
9. No one noticed the theft until morning.
10. The map was soiled and torn.

EXERCISE B: Writing Subjects and Predicates. Supply a simple subject for each blank underlined once. Supply a simple predicate for each blank underlined twice.

EXAMPLES: The ___*canary*___ refused to sing.
Inspector Low ___*solved*___ the mystery.

1. Chickens _____ from eggs.
2. The _____ gave the speeder a ticket.
3. Luis _____ a fine for the overdue book.
4. The _____ was a great surprise.
5. The burglar probably _____ through the window.

10.2 Complete Subjects and Predicates

The complete subject of a sentence is the simple subject and the words related to it. The complete predicate is the verb and the words related to it. In the chart below, complete subjects and predicates are labeled. Each simple subject is underlined once, and each simple predicate is underlined twice.

COMPLETE SUBJECTS AND COMPLETE PREDICATES
Complete Subjects/Complete Predicates
The shipwrecked <u>sailors</u> <u>lived</u> in a cave.
Several <u>students</u> in our class <u>entered</u> the poster contest.
<u>Michelle</u> <u>won</u> first prize.
An unidentified <u>aircraft</u> <u>approached</u> the airport.

EXERCISE A: Recognizing Complete Subjects and Predicates. Draw a vertical line between the complete subject and the complete predicate of each sentence below.

EXAMPLE: Animals in fables | act like human beings.

1. A shiny new bicycle stood outside the door.
2. The third problem is a little tricky.
3. The first Monday in September is Labor Day.
4. My older brother earns money doing odd jobs.
5. The first radio station in the United States was KDKA in Pittsburgh.
6. The waiter accepted the tip with a grateful smile.
7. A few water lilies floated on the pond.
8. Boats of every description joined in the rescue.
9. A friend from the old neighborhood was visiting Ellen.
10. This toy requires some assembly.

EXERCISE B: Identifying Complete and Simple Subjects and Predicates. Draw a vertical line between the complete subject and the complete predicate. Underline the simple subject once and the simple predicate twice.

EXAMPLE: The <u>dog</u> in the manger | <u>kept</u> the cows away.

1. The tanker was slowly breaking to pieces on the rocks.
2. The youngest of the three brothers has the best voice.
3. The manager of the Otters argued angrily with the umpire.
4. A large crocodile snoozed in the mud near the shore.
5. The hedge in front of the house concealed the street.
6. The drawer of the teller's desk contained only a few travel folders.
7. That girl in the trenchcoat is a reporter.
8. A simple majority is needed for passage.
9. Few of the spectators stayed until the end of the game.
10. Her sincere apology satisfied everyone.

10.3 Compound Subjects and Predicates

A compound subject is two or more simple subjects that are related to the same verb. A compound predicate is two or more verbs that are related to the same subject.

COMPOUND SUBJECTS AND PREDICATES	
Compound Subjects	**Compound Predicates**
<u>Trolls</u> and <u>ogres</u> are fairytale creatures.	The big dog <u>lay</u> down and <u>rolled</u> over.
<u>Sheila</u> or <u>Paula</u> will take the message.	Most students <u>walk</u> or <u>ride</u> bikes to school.

EXERCISE A: Recognizing Compound Subjects. Underline the simple subjects that make up each compound subject below.

EXAMPLE: An <u>apple</u> or a <u>banana</u> makes a good snack.

1. Trucks and buses may not use the left-hand lane.
2. A teacher or a parent accompanied each group.
3. An encyclopedia or a dictionary should have that information.
4. The director and her assistant hold the tryouts.
5. Before moving here, Rachel and her sister lived in New York City.
6. Neither threats nor pleas could change Peter's mind.
7. Bottles and glass jars belong in this bin.
8. A judge, justice-of-the-peace, or ship captain can marry a couple.
9. Salad and dessert are not included in the special.
10. A doctor or nurse is present at all times.

EXERCISE B: Recognizing Compound Predicates. Underline twice the verbs that make up each compound predicate below.

EXAMPLE: The speedboat <u>capsized</u> and <u>sank</u>.

1. Trees swayed and bent in the high winds.
2. The spectators stood up and cheered.
3. Many employees jog or do exercises at lunchtime.
4. Beatrix Potter wrote and illustrated her stories.
5. Customers can now deposit or withdraw money by machine.
6. The company repairs or replaces all defective watches.
7. Jeff sanded the surface lightly and wiped it clean.
8. From four to five, campers rest or write letters.
9. Volunteers stuff, address, and stamp envelopes.
10. The audience booed and hissed the villain.

10.4 Hard-to-Find Subjects

The subject of a command or request is understood to be the word *you.* In questions, the subject follows the verb or is located between a helping verb and the main verb. The words *there* and *here* are never subjects.

LOCATING HARD-TO-FIND SUBJECTS	
Commands or Requests	**How the Sentences Are Understood**
Listen!	You listen!
Turn to page 24.	You turn to page 24.
Mike, please fasten your seatbelt.	Mike, you please fasten your seatbelt.
Questions	**Questions Changed to Statements**
Is it bigger than a house?	It is bigger than a house.
Has the play started?	The play has started.
When are they leaving?	They are leaving when.
Sentences with There or Here	**Reworded with Subjects First**
There goes the champ.	The champ goes there.
Here are the tickets.	The tickets are here.
There is a fly in my soup.	A fly is in my soup.

EXERCISE A: Recognizing Hard-to-Find Subjects. Underline the subject in each sentence below.

EXAMPLE: There are chickens in the trees.

1. Where are my binoculars?
2. Here is the place to turn.
3. There are two pairs of twins in my class.
4. Does a cat always land on its feet?
5. When does the baseball season start?
6. Are cameras allowed inside the museum?
7. There goes our last chance to win.
8. Are there more nails in that can?
9. Here is my most valuable stamp.
10. There is a letter for you on the table.

EXERCISE B: Identifying the Subject of a Command or Request. Write the subject of each sentence in the blank at the right. Put a caret (∧) where the subject belongs in the sentence.

EXAMPLE: Mark, ∧ please lend me your ruler. __*(you)*__

1. Jill, hand me those photographs, please. _____
2. Now open to the last page of your test booklet. _____
3. Do not stick a knife or fork into the toaster. _____
4. Wendy, watch the baby for a moment, please. _____
5. John and Aaron, stop that roughhousing this minute! _____

11.1 Direct Objects

A direct object is a noun or pronoun that appears with an action verb and receives the action of the verb.

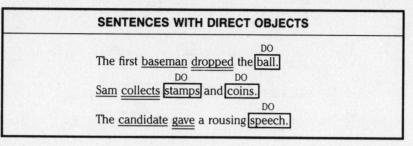

SENTENCES WITH DIRECT OBJECTS

The first baseman dropped the ball.

Sam collects stamps and coins.

The candidate gave a rousing speech.

EXERCISE A: Finding Direct Objects. Draw a box around the direct object in each sentence below. If there are two or more direct objects in a sentence, draw a box around each one.

EXAMPLE: The mechanic checked the brakes and oil.

1. The pianist played several encores.
2. An animal often warns other animals of danger.
3. Sanchez hit the ball over the right-field fence.
4. Mrs. Lewis greeted each guest at the door.
5. The magician passed his wand slowly over the box.
6. Mr. Kelly grows orchids as a hobby.
7. Buckling up in seatbelts saves lives.
8. Stephanie studied the blueprints and the directions.
9. The magazine publishes articles and a few stories.
10. The boy cut his foot on a sharp rock.

EXERCISE B: Writing Sentences with Direct Objects. Add words to each sentence beginning below to make a complete sentence. Be sure that the complete sentence contains a direct object.

EXAMPLE: Jennifer borrowed ___a book from the library___.

1. In science today, we studied _____.
2. We all enjoyed _____.
3. At first, the detective suspected _____.
4. For a snack, I like _____.
5. The teacher complimented _____.
6. The treasure-hunters discovered _____.
7. Have you ever read _____?
8. The lifeguard rescued _____.
9. The letter carrier delivered _____.
10. Before the game, a soprano sang _____.

11.2 Indirect Objects

An indirect object is a noun or pronoun usually located between an action verb and a direct object. It tells the person or thing something is given to or done for.

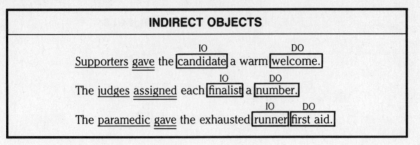

INDIRECT OBJECTS

IO   DO
Supporters gave the candidate a warm welcome.

IO   DO
The judges assigned each finalist a number.

IO   DO
The paramedic gave the exhausted runner first aid.

EXERCISE A: Recognizing Indirect Objects. Draw a box around each indirect object. If there are two or more indirect objects, draw a box around each one.

EXAMPLE: The owner offered Carla a reward.

1. Heather built her rabbit a new hutch.
2. A police officer showed the tourists the way.
3. The owner of the cheese shop offered Clare and me a free sample.
4. The librarian brought us the old newspaper.
5. Gail wrote her aunt a thank-you note.
6. The judges awarded Alicia first prize.
7. The principal gave Tom and Alex a stern warning.
8. Henry brought his mother a bouquet of flowers.
9. Mr. Dithers promised Dagwood a raise.
10. The Bemaks sent us a postcard from Greece.

EXERCISE B: Writing Sentences with Indirect Objects. Rewrite each sentence below, changing the underlined prepositional phrase into an indirect object.

EXAMPLE: We fed peanuts to the elephant.
              We fed the elephant peanuts.

1. The mayor gave a medal to Nicole.

   _____

2. The class sent canned goods to the charitable organization.

   _____

3. My uncle found a summer job for me.

   _____

4. I wrote a letter to the author of the book.

   _____

5. The letter carrier brought a letter for me.

   _____

12.1 Predicate Nouns

A predicate noun is a noun that appears with a subject and a linking verb. It renames or identifies the subject.

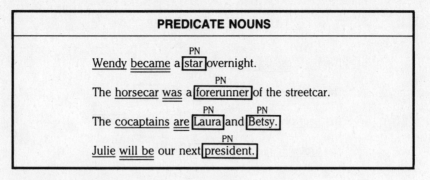

PREDICATE NOUNS

Wendy became a star overnight.

The horsecar was a forerunner of the streetcar.

The cocaptains are Laura and Betsy.

Julie will be our next president.

EXERCISE A: Recognizing Predicate Nouns. Underline each predicate noun.

EXAMPLE: The turtle is a kind of reptile.

1. Whales and porpoises are mammals.
2. My favorite vegetables are corn and spinach.
3. The unicorn is a mythical beast.
4. After years of study, Dana became a doctor.
5. The mascot of the Navy team is a goat.
6. The former rivals became good friends.
7. John will probably remain team captain.
8. The runners-up were Lisa and Mark.
9. Eventually, the liquid became ice cream.
10. Leslie has remained my best friend.

EXERCISE B: More Work with Predicate Nouns. Underline the predicate noun(s) in each sentence. In the space, write the word the predicate noun(s) rename or identify.

EXAMPLE: Hurricanes are tropical storms. ___*hurricanes*___

1. Today's speaker is a nationally known columnist. _____
2. Lewis and Clark were famous American explorers. _____
3. Maurice Sendak is an author and an illustrator. _____
4. Australia is a continent and a country. _____
5. The first woman astronaut was Valentina V. Tereshkova. _____
6. The number with 100 zeros is a googol. _____
7. Computer programming is a fast-growing career. _____
8. After a close election, Mr. Ramos remains the mayor. _____
9. John F. Kennedy became President at the age of 43. _____
10. Soccer is David's favorite sport. _____

12.2 Predicate Adjectives

A predicate adjective is an adjective that appears with a subject and a linking verb. It describes or modifies the subject of the sentence.

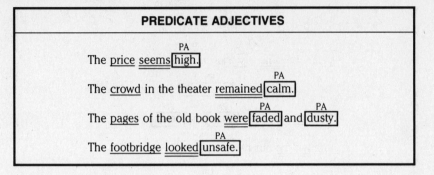

EXERCISE A: Recognizing Predicate Adjectives. Underline each predicate adjective. Then circle the subject it modifies.

EXAMPLE: The new (law) is <u>unfair</u> to dogs.

1. Norman's plan sounds impractical.
2. It grows dark rapidly in the forest.
3. Today's crossword puzzle looks quite hard.
4. The defendant's story sounded fishy.
5. Most of the runners looked weary at the finish line.
6. This milk smells sour.
7. Sugar maples turn yellow in the fall.
8. The water feels cold at first.
9. The bank teller became suspicious.
10. The day was hot and muggy.

EXERCISE B: Using Predicate Adjectives in Sentences. Complete each sentence below by adding an appropriate predicate adjective.

EXAMPLE: Skateboarding can be ___*dangerous*___.

1. In the fall, the days grow _____.
2. This album is _____.
3. A good adventure movie is _____.
4. After exercise, a shower feels _____.
5. Metal buttons on a uniform should be _____.
6. Pretzels usually taste _____.
7. Some scenes in a horror movie will probably be _____.
8. After winning an important game, a player feels _____.
9. Popcorn smells _____.
10. Velvet feels _____.

13.1 Four Kinds of Sentences

There are four kinds of sentences: declarative, interrogative, imperative, and exclamatory.

FOUR KINDS OF SENTENCES	
Kinds of Sentences	**Examples**
Declarative	Whitcomb L. Judson invented the zipper.
Interrogative	Who invented the zipper?
Imperative	Lend me your book about inventors.
Exclamatory	What a lot of inventions there are!

EXERCISE A: Identifying the Four Kinds of Sentences. Identify each sentence below as *declarative, interrogative, imperative,* or *exclamatory.*

EXAMPLE: Add the milk to the dry ingredients slowly. ___*imperative*___

1. Who was the first woman astronaut? _____

2. Buckle your seatbelt even for short trips. _____

3. Please put the stamped envelopes in this box. _____

4. You must be joking! _____

5. What a thrill that ride was! _____

6. In 1776, there were 53 newspapers in London. _____

7. Who were the first people to use paper money? _____

8. Insert the diskette in this slot. _____

9. Insects outnumber people by millions to one. _____

10. What an amazing story that is! _____

EXERCISE B: Choosing the Correct End Mark for Sentences. On the line provided, supply an appropriate end mark for each sentence.

EXAMPLE: English has many interesting names for groups of animals___.___

1. Give us some examples _____

2. Well, a group of lions is a pride _____

3. What is a group of leopards called _____

4. Have you ever heard of a leap of leopards _____

5. What a great name that is for those cats _____

6. A gam is a group of whales _____

7. Then what is a pod _____

8. Look up both words in a dictionary, please _____

9. Either noun can be used for whales _____

10. One is just as weird as the other _____

13.2 Basic Sentence Patterns

Basic sentence patterns describe how subjects, verbs, and complements are arranged in a sentence.

BASIC SENTENCE PATTERNS	
Patterns	**Examples**
S-V	The crowd roared.
S-V-DO	Julie read her horoscope.
S-V-IO-DO	Annie gave her dog a bath.
S-LV-PN	The caterpillar became a butterfly.
S-LV-PA	This gum tastes sour.

EXERCISE A: Identifying Basic Sentence Patterns. Identify each sentence below by pattern: S-V, S-V-DO, S-V-IO-DO, S-LV-PN, S-LV-PA.

EXAMPLE: The pitcher threw a fast ball. _S-V-DO_

1. High winds battered the island. _____

2. Mr. Salvin gave my paper an *A*. _____

3. Kathy sent her grandmother a birthday card. _____

4. That song sounds familiar. _____

5. The rain stopped. _____

6. A group of cats is a clutter. _____

7. Sam shrugged his shoulders. _____

8. Coach Barrows was optimistic. _____

9. The colt became a famous racehorse. _____

10. The flood waters rose rapidly. _____

EXERCISE B: Using Basic Sentence Patterns. Write a sentence of your own for each of the patterns in parentheses. Label each subject, verb, and complement in your sentences.

EXAMPLE: S-V-DO _Jack lost his lunch money_.

1. (S-V-IO-DO) _____

2. (S-LV-PA) _____

3. (S-LV-PN) _____

4. (S-V) _____

5. (S-V-DO) _____

13.3 | Diagraming Sentences

A diagram shows how the parts of a sentence are related.

DECLARATIVE

Snow was falling.

Snow	was falling

INTERROGATIVE

Do you ski?

you	Do ski

IMPERATIVE

Listen!

(you)	Listen

EXERCISE A: Diagraming Declarative and Imperative Sentences. Diagram each sentence below. Use the models above if you need to.

1. Snakes crawl.

2. Stop!

3. Birds were singing.

EXERCISE B: Diagraming Interrogative Sentences. Diagram each sentence below. Refer to the model if you need to.

1. Are you listening?

2. Has he finished.?

14.1 Phrases That Act as Adjectives

An adjective phrase is a prepositional phrase that modifies a noun or pronoun.

ADJECTIVE PHRASES

The shops *in the mall* are still open. (modifies a noun)
The manager wants someone *with experience.* (modifies a pronoun)

EXERCISE A: Finding Adjective Phrases. Underline the adjective phrase in each sentence. Circle the noun or pronoun it modifies.

EXAMPLE: (Teams) in the junior baseball league have ten players.

1. The main character in the story is a young boy.
2. He is a visitor from another planet.
3. Part of the treasure map is missing.
4. The road along the coastline has the best views.
5. Several of the eggs are cracked.
6. The sign on the bench said "WET PAINT."
7. I'm reading a book about the Pony Express.
8. I would like a bike with ten speeds.
9. The gate to the playground is locked.
10. The notebook with the plaid cover is mine.

EXERCISE B: Using Adjective Phrases. Write a sentence of your own using the prepositional phrase in parentheses as an adjective phrase. Circle the noun or pronoun that the phrase modifies in your sentence.

EXAMPLE: (with the closed shutters) _The (house) with the closed shutters is spooky._

1. (in the meadow) _____
2. (through the woods) _____
3. (from another country) _____
4. (about computers) _____
5. (of stamps) _____

14.2 Phrases That Act as Adverbs

An adverb phrase is a prepositional phrase that modifies a verb, an adjective, or an adverb.

ADVERB PHRASES
Camera club meets *on Wednesdays*. (modifies a verb)
Paul was happy *about his home run*. (modifies an adjective)
He arrived too late *for dinner*. (modifies an adverb)

EXERCISE A: Recognizing Adverb Phrases. Underline the adverb phrase in each sentence below. Circle the word the phrase modifies.

EXAMPLE: Cindy (borrowed) lunch money <u>from the office.</u>

1. The soldiers crossed the river in small boats.
2. The library closes early on Saturdays.
3. Michelle delivers papers after school.
4. Water boils at 100° Celsius.
5. The coat was too big for the little boy.
6. Kevin plays the trumpet in the school band.
7. The children were curious about the large package.
8. The trail led along the rim of the canyon.
9. Sam practices for an hour every day.
10. We started hiking early in the morning.

EXERCISE B: Using Adverb Phrases. Write a sentence of your own using each of the prepositional phrases in parentheses as an adverb phrase. Circle the word the phrase modifies in your sentence.

EXAMPLE: (for his age) ___*Steve seems* (tall) *for his age.*___

1. (through the window) _____
2. (after the storm) _____
3. (into the fishbowl) _____
4. (to the speaker) _____
5. (by the six points) _____

14.3 Phrases That Rename, Identify, or Explain

An appositive phrase renames, identifies, or explains the noun with which it appears.

APPOSITIVE PHRASES

The equator, <u>an imaginary line</u>, separates the Northern and Southern Hemispheres.

James Madison, <u>our fourth President</u>, was the first to live in the White House.

The Adventures of Huckleberry Finn, <u>Mark Twain's most famous novel</u>, was published in 1884.

EXERCISE A: Finding Appositive Phrases. Underline the appositive phrase in each sentence. Circle the noun or pronoun it identifies or explains.

EXAMPLE: (Alfred Nobel,) the inventor of dynamite, invented the Nobel Prizes.

1. The eohippus, a small hoofed mammal, was the ancestor of the horse.
2. Dave, a strong swimmer, works as a lifeguard in the summers.
3. The damaged plane, a Boeing 727, landed safely.
4. The lighthouse, a landmark for sailors, is nearly two hundred years old.
5. Enrico Caruso, a famous opera tenor, had an amazing voice.
6. Ms. Geering, the next mayor, has promised many reforms.
7. The blue whale, the largest mammal on earth, can weigh up to 115 tons.
8. Mr. Amati, our neighbor, makes violins as a hobby.
9. Either of two alphabets may be used in writing Serbo-Croatian, the language of Yugoslavia.
10. The wallet should be returned to me, the rightful owner.

EXERCISE B: Using Appositive Phrases. Write a sentence of your own in which you use each phrase below as an appositive phrase. Circle the noun or pronoun that the appositive phrase identifies or explains.

EXAMPLE: (my favorite rock group)
(The Wrecking Crew,) *my favorite rock group, will be at the Orpheum on Friday.*

1. (our next-door neighbor) _____

   _____

2. (my favorite snack) _____

   _____

3. (a famous rock singer) _____

   _____

4. (the school principal) _____

   _____

5. (our state capital) _____

   _____

14.4 Diagraming Phrases

A prepositional phrase is diagramed to show how it relates the object of the preposition to another word in the sentence. The preposition is written on a slanted line joined to the word the phrase modifies. The object is written on a horizontal line. One-word modifiers are placed on a slanted line below the words they modify.

ADJECTIVE PHRASE	ADVERB PHRASE
The flowers *in the windowbox* are dying.	The boat arrives early *in the morning*.

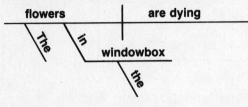 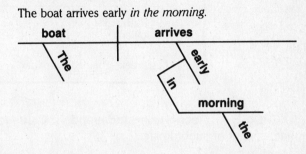

To diagram an appositive phrase, put the most important noun in the phrase in parentheses and place it next to the noun it renames, identifies, or explains. Place modifiers beneath the noun.

APPOSITIVE PHRASE

John, *the team captain*, is batting now.

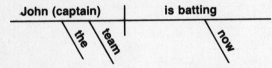

EXERCISE A: Diagraming Adjective and Adverb Phrases. Correctly diagram each sentence.

1. The team with the red shirts is winning.

2. The door closed with a bang.

3. The girl behind me was speaking in a whisper.

EXERCISE B: Diagraming Appositive Phrases. Correctly diagram each sentence.

1. Ulysses, the Greek leader, was plotting.

2. Ellen, the runner-up, smiled happily.

15.1 Recognizing Independent Clauses

A clause is a group of words that contains both a subject and a verb. An independent clause has a subject and verb and can stand alone as a complete sentence. A subordinate clause has a subject and verb but cannot stand alone as a complete sentence.

CLAUSES	
Independent Clauses	**Subordinate Clauses**
The library has a new computer.	if the door is not closed
Last week, it rained every day.	after the bell rings

EXERCISE A: Recognizing Independent Clauses. In the space provided, identify each clause as independent or subordinate.

EXAMPLE: the last scene scared many viewers ___*independent*___

1. the ancient Egyptians worshipped cats _____

2. who have some experience _____

3. after the concert has begun _____

4. some trains travel at 120 miles per hour _____

5. the map of Thailand is shaped like an elephant's head _____

6. until the last out has been made _____

7. although Jamie did not expect to win _____

8. before the runner could get to first base _____

9. Ms. Maloney teaches science _____

10. we were waiting for the bus _____

EXERCISE B: Writing Independent Clauses. Write each independent clause from Exercise A, adding a capital at the beginning and a period at the end.

EXAMPLE: The last scene scared many viewers.

1. _____

2. _____

3. _____

4. _____

5. _____

15.2 Forming Compound Sentences

A compound sentence is made up of two or more independent clauses. The clauses are usually joined by a comma and a coordinating conjunction *(and, but, for, nor, or, so,* or *yet)*. The clauses of a compound sentence may also be joined with a semicolon (;).

COMPOUND SENTENCES
The sky cleared, and the rain stopped.
The food at Casey's is good, but the service is terrible.
Both doors must be shut, or the elevator will not operate.
Lou wasn't ready for the big test; he had not studied at all.

EXERCISE A: Identifying the Parts of Compound Sentences. Underline the subjects of the clauses of each compound sentence once. Underline the verbs of the clauses twice. Circle the coordinating conjunction or semicolon that joins the clauses.

EXAMPLE: The boy cried "Wolf!" no one paid any attention.

1. The water looked inviting, but it was very cold.
2. Leaves were turning, and the geese were flying south.
3. The recipe calls for salt, but I don't use any.
4. We expected rain, for all of the forecasts had predicted it.
5. Sharon could not make a decision; so much depended on the outcome.
6. We must score six runs, or the Renegades will win.
7. No one walked unnoticed down Maple Lane, for Mrs. Lewis was always at her window.
8. The work was dangerous, but it paid well.
9. Scott didn't expect to win the broad jump, yet he still entered.
10. We have to pay for the soda anyway, so we might as well drink it.

EXERCISE B: Writing Compound Sentences. Combine each pair of independent clauses into a compound sentence. Use a comma and the coordinating conjunction shown in brackets.

EXAMPLE: The ship sank. The passengers were all safe.   [but]
   The ship sank, but the passengers were all safe.

1. Cinderella married the prince. They lived happily ever after.   [and]

   _____

2. The inventor had many disappointments. He didn't give up. [but]

   _____

3. Voters must register. They cannot vote.   [or]

   _____

4. My sister wants to graduate early. She is going to summer school.   [so]

   _____

5. We expected a storm. The barometer was falling rapidly.   [for]

   _____

15.3 Diagraming Compound Sentences

The clauses of a compound sentence are diagramed separately, one under the other. They are connected by a dotted line that looks like a step. The coordinating conjunction or semicolon is written on the step. Notice that a direct object is placed after the verb with a short line separating them.

COMPOUND SENTENCES

Jason likes football, but I prefer baseball.

We must start soon, or we will arrive too late.

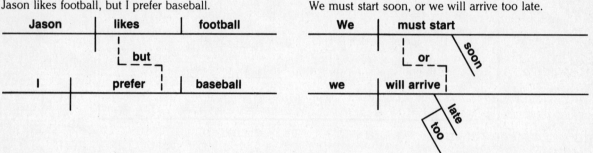

EXERCISE A: Diagraming Compound Sentences. Diagram each of the following compound sentences.

1. Adults must have a child with them, or they cannot enter the zoo.

2. The plane developed engine trouble, and the pilot made a forced landing.

3. The police freed the suspect, for they believed his story.

EXERCISE B: Interpreting Diagrams. Write the compound sentence represented by each diagram below.

1.

2.

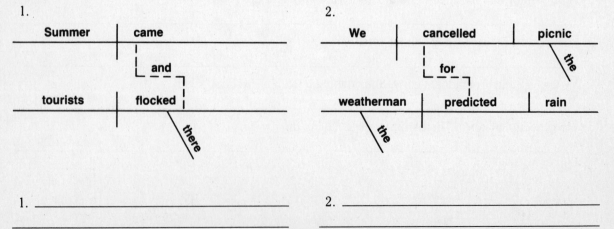

1. _____

2. _____

_____

_____

16.1 Recognizing Fragments

A fragment is a group of words that does not express a complete thought.

Fragments	What Is Missing
The damaged moving van.	a verb
Waited for an answer.	a subject
Guests strolling on the beach.	a complete verb
On the deck.	a subject and a verb
If it stops raining.	an independent clause

EXERCISE A: Recognizing Fragments. After each group of words, write *fragment* or *sentence*, whichever describes the word group.

EXAMPLE: In the middle of a quiet conversation. ___*fragment*___

1. Who always arrives at school half an hour early. _____

2. Several customers still waiting to be seated. _____

3. The principal asked me to step into his office. _____

4. In some bushes near the bike rack on the playground. _____

5. If it rains tomorrow, the picnic will be indoors. _____

6. The pants shrank. _____

7. Depended on the success of the mission. _____

8. A mysterious black limousine with smoked windows. _____

9. The bus finally got to the village. _____

10. A few customers complained loudly. _____

EXERCISE B: Identifying What Is Missing from Fragments. Copy the fragments you found in Exercise A, including the number of each. After the fragment, write what is missing: *a verb, a subject, a complete verb, a subject and a verb,* or *an independent clause.*

EXAMPLE: ___*In the middle of a quiet conversation.   a subject and a verb*___

1. _____

2. _____

3. _____

4. _____

5. _____

16.2 Correcting Fragments

To correct a fragment, use one of these methods: (1) Connect the fragment to a nearby sentence. (2) Add the necessary words to change the fragment into a sentence.

<table>
<tr><td colspan="1">CORRECTING FRAGMENTS</td></tr>
</table>

CORRECTING FRAGMENTS
Connecting Fragments to Nearby Sentences
A few customers stood at the door. *Waiting to be seated.* (fragment)   A few customers stood at the door waiting to be seated. (joined to sentence)   *Although the work was dangerous.* The pay was good. (fragment)   Although the work was dangerous, the pay was good. (attached sentence)
Adding Necessary Words to Fragments
During the scariest part of the movie. (fragment)   I closed my eyes during the scariest part of the movie. (sentence)   *Depended on the success of the mission.* (fragment)   Victory depended on the success of the mission. (sentence)

EXERCISE A: Connecting Fragments to Nearby Sentences. Correct each fragment by connecting it to a nearby sentence. Write only the sentence containing the corrected fragment.

EXAMPLE: She vanished. <u>In a moment</u>. No one ever saw her again.
        She vanished in a moment.

1. A ship sailed into the harbor. <u>Flying a strange flag</u>. Everyone was curious.

_____

2. You may use my binoculars. <u>If you are careful with them</u>. Otherwise you can't.

_____

3. We got off the boat. <u>With a few seconds to spare</u>. Then it went down.

_____

4. The magician found the card. <u>Right in my pocket</u>! It was amazing.

_____

5. We finished our set. Then we took a swim. <u>While you finished your set</u>.

_____

EXERCISE B: Adding Necessary Words to Change Fragments to Sentences. Change the following fragments into complete sentences by adding the necessary words.

EXAMPLE: A crowd of curious passers-by.
        A crowd of curious passers-by gathered to watch the artist.

1. A parking space too small for our car.

_____

2. A few minutes before midnight.

_____

3. Carrying one important passenger.

_____

4. People hoping to get a letter.

_____

5. Elected unanimously.

_____

17.1 Recognizing Run-Ons

A run-on sentence is two or more sentences written as if they were one sentence.

RUN-ON SENTENCES

Cheetahs run very fast in fact, they are the fastest animal. (no punctuation after *fast*)
Large rain forests are located in South America and central Africa, rain falls there every day. (Just a comma separates two independent clauses.)
The nose does two jobs in breathing, it warms the air and cleans it. (just a comma after *breathing*)
It's hard to choose clothes there are so many things I like. (No punctuation mark separates the two independent clauses.)

EXERCISE A: Recognizing Run-Ons. After each word group, write *sentence* or *run-on*, whichever describes that word group.

EXAMPLE: The Wright brothers made the first successful powered flight, it lasted 12 seconds.
_____*run-on*_____

1. The governor was a fine speaker she gave a rousing keynote speech. _____

2. Students objected to the plan, and the teachers didn't like it either. _____

3. The soldiers were tired, they had marched all day. _____

4. Charles locked the windows and doors, then he turned out the lights. _____

5. The new vaccine seems promising, but it has not yet been fully tested. _____

6. The job paid less than John had hoped, yet he decided to take it. _____

7. The boys had no ticket stubs, they were asked to leave. _____

8. Cathy is the new president, and Mark is the treasurer. _____

9. Do not cook the stew too long, or the meat will get stringy. _____

10. The sign was unnecessary, no one went near the haunted house. _____

EXERCISE B: Analyzing Run-On Sentences. Copy the run-on sentences you found in Exercise A, including the number of each. Then circle the place where the two sentences are incorrectly joined.

EXAMPLE: The Wright brothers made the first successful powered flight⊙it lasted 12 seconds.

_____

_____

_____

_____

_____

17.2 Correcting Run-On Sentences

Use one of the following ways to correct run-ons.

END MARK
The crowd was amazed they had never seen anything like it. (run-on) The crowd was amazed. They had never seen anything like it. (corrected)
COMMAS AND SUBORDINATING CONJUNCTION
We built a big fire, the rescue party saw the smoke. (run-on) We built a big fire, and the rescue party saw the smoke. (correction)
SEMICOLON
Water makes temperatures even, it neither heats nor cools as fast as land. (run-on) Water makes temperatures even; it neither heats nor cools as fast as land. (correction)
ONE COMPLEX SENTENCE
We tried the plan, it was risky. (run-on) We tried the plan even though it was risky. (corrected)

EXERCISE A: Preparing to Correct Run-Ons. If a word group below is a run-on sentence, insert a caret (∧) between the two sentences or independent clauses. If a sentence is correct, write *C* after it.

EXAMPLE: At the equator the sun's rays are direct,∧they are strong and hot. _____

1. Rain-forest people live in villages, and their houses are small and dim. _____

2. Alligators lay their eggs in the mud the sun hatches them. _____

3. Cooking is easy, a cookbook is all you need. _____

4. Many people collect baseball cards; some cards are very valuable. _____

5. The first playing cards came from China they were used to tell fortunes. _____

6. Most tourists view the canyon from the rim, but a few travel to its floor on donkeys. _____

7. Yellowstone Park is our oldest National Park it opened in 1872. _____

8. Regular mail takes several days, but express mail arrives the next day. _____

9. Tomatoes are expensive to ship, for they bruise easily. _____

10. The bus driver refused to drive so the passengers got off angrily. _____

EXERCISE B: Correcting Run-Ons. Rewrite five run-on sentences from Exercise A. Use each method of rewriting noted in the chart at least once.

EXAMPLE: At the equator the sun's rays are direct; they are strong and hot.

_____

_____

_____

_____

_____

18.1 Formal English

Formal English is a serious kind of writing used when writing about important information. People generally choose to write formal English when they write business letters, school reports, formal speeches, and other significant information.

RULES FOR WRITING FORMAL ENLGISH	
Use no contractions	The guests *will not* arrive until noon.
Use no slang	We should leave. (rather than *Let's split*.)
Use the pronoun *one*	*One* should be prepared for emergencies.
Use straightforward sentences	The birds migrated south.

EXERCISE A: Recognizing Formal English. In each set of parentheses, circle the more formal word or phrase.

EXAMPLE: The officer (did not, didn't) issue us a ticket.

1. Marian seems (stuck-up, indifferent).
2. The hikers are responsible for their own (equipment, gear).
3. (One, you) should call in advance for reservations.
4. The doctor (can't, cannot) come to the phone right now.
5. My friend feels (under the weather, ill).
6. (You, one) should study hard for any test.
7. It is polite for (one, you) to take small bites and eat slowly.
8. (I've got to run, I must leave) before noon.
9. (Hey, Excuse me), how far is Amber Avenue from here?
10. The rain came down (heavily, in buckets).

EXERCISE B: Using Formal English. In each sentence, an underlined word or phrase is not considered formal English. Rewrite it to make it more formal.

EXAMPLE: Mary passed her test <u>with flying colors</u>.   *easily*

1. We should <u>turn in</u> for the night. _____
2. <u>You'll</u> never learn, Bill, unless you practice. _____
3. The settlers <u>couldn't</u> continue without food. _____
4. A neighbor <u>dropped by</u> with some homemade jam. _____
5. That's a <u>crazy</u> outfit that she is wearing. _____
6. Martin is a <u>slick</u> soccer player. _____
7. I will <u>jot</u> his telephone number down. _____
8. The astronauts <u>couldn't</u> complete the experiment. _____
9. When the President speaks, <u>you</u> should listen. _____
10. We had better <u>hit the road</u>. _____

18.2 Writing Informal English

Informal English is used by the same people who speak and write formal English, but it is generally used in more casual, everyday situations. Most newspaper reports, friendly letters, or diaries are written in informal English.

RULES FOR WRITING INFORMAL ENGLISH	
You May Use:	**Example**
Contractions	*You'll* win that championship game.
Popular expressions	I *bombed* that test.
The pronoun *you*	*You* can never tell about the weather.

EXERCISE A: Recognizing Informal English. Write *informal* or *formal* on the line after each sentence.

EXAMPLE: I dragged my feet. ___*informal*___

1. One should read the newspapers to stay current on the news. _____

2. We'll never finish this in time. _____

3. This dress looks dumb on me. _____

4. The President's speech was clearly heard. _____

5. Condors live in South America and California. _____

6. That crook won't get away with it. _____

7. Let's not debate this all night. _____

8. One must always read instructions thoroughly. _____

9. We'll tackle this problem tomorrow. _____

10. I'm roasted from all this hot weather. _____

EXERCISE B: Writing Informal English. Each sentence below is written in formal English. Rewrite it so that it is informal.

EXAMPLE: I heard the entire story. ___*I got the whole scoop.*___

1. One can never be too sure. _____

2. Bob will always be my friend. _____

3. The store will not reduce its prices. _____

4. He will work in the yard. _____

5. One should not waste food. _____

6. She will attend the party. _____

7. One should not underestimate his enemies. _____

8. I shall ride my bicycle over. _____

9. The athlete was exhausted. _____

10. He will telephone you tomorrow. _____

19.1 Regular Verbs

Regular verbs form the tenses following a regular, consistent pattern. The four parts used to form the tenses are the present, present participle, past, and past participle.

PRINCIPAL PARTS OF REGULAR VERBS			
Present	**Present Participle**	**Past**	**Past Participle**
laugh	(am) laughing	laughed	(have) laughed
offer	(am) offering	offered	(have) offered
fade	(is) fading	faded	(has) faded

EXERCISE A: Using Regular Verbs. Look at the tense of the regular verb underlined in each sentence. If it is correct, write *C* in the blank provided. If it is incorrect, write the correct tense in the blank.

EXAMPLE: Yesterday, I <u>am wishing</u> for a bike.   *__wished__*

1. Last week, I <u>have painted</u> the fence. _____

2. The artist <u>will donate</u> a watercolor. _____

3. The group is <u>lacked</u> money for its next project. _____

4. I <u>will present</u> the awards last night. _____

5. We <u>are watching</u> a baseball game right now. _____

6. Yesterday, the band <u>will practice</u> three hours. _____

7. In a moment, the horse <u>jump</u> over a hurdle. _____

8. After dinner, I <u>will taste</u> the chocolate cake. _____

9. After the job was done, we <u>will divide</u> the profits. _____

10. I <u>love</u> chocolate chip cookies. _____

EXERCISE B: More Work with Regular Verbs. On the line provided, write the correct form of the verb in parentheses.

EXAMPLE: We (race) down the street just now.   *__raced__*

1. Liz is (brush) her hair. _____

2. Rich Little (imitate) famous people. _____

3. He has (fill) the tank with gasoline. _____

4. When I was little, I (hate) spinach. _____

5. My mother is (attend) the performance. _____

6. The school has (close) the library for the day. _____

7. He will (show) us some magic tricks. _____

8. We have (play) lots of card games. _____

9. The gardener has (spray) the lawn for weeds. _____

10. I am (salute) the flag. _____

19.2 Irregular Verbs

A small group of verbs are called irregular verbs. These verbs differ from regular verbs in the way they form the tenses. Irregular verbs do not form the participle by adding -ed or -d to the present.

IRREGULAR VERBS WITH THE SAME PAST AND PAST PARTICIPLE			
Present	**Present Participle**	**Past**	**Past Participle**
shoot	(am) shooting	shot	(have) shot
wind	(am) winding	wound	(have) wound
feel	(am) feeling	felt	(have) felt

EXERCISE A: Using Irregular Verbs. If the irregular verb underlined in each sentence is correct, write *C* in the blank. If the irregular verb is incorrect, write the correct tense in the blank.

EXAMPLE: I <u>leaded</u> the group on the hike. ___*led*___

1. Today we <u>are bought</u> a new car. _____

2. The mosquitos <u>are stinging</u> us constantly. _____

3. The car <u>spun</u> out of control. _____

4. I <u>shot</u> at the target tomorrow. _____

5. I <u>will hold</u> your ice cream for you. _____

6. Yesterday, Mike <u>has got</u> some good fish. _____

7. In the past, I <u>have</u> even more baseball cards. _____

8. Nick <u>is having</u> second thoughts. _____

9. Last night, I <u>am catching</u> a fly ball. _____

10. Yesterday morning I <u>learn</u> about the Civil War. _____

EXERCISE B: More Work with Irregular Verbs. In the blank, write the correct verb tense for the irregular verb in parentheses.

EXAMPLE: The company has (build) many homes in the area. ___*built*___

1. They (buy) a cake for his birthday. _____

2. My father is (lose) his hair. _____

3. Our guests have (bring) their vacation pictures. _____

4. Are you (get) what you need? _____

5. We are (find) the crowds tiresome. _____

6. Have you (pay) the bill? _____

7. The police (catch) the suspect. _____

8. I (hold) the monkey while my picture was taken. _____

9. Yesterday, I (swing) and missed. _____

10. We (stick) to the original agreement. _____

19.3 More Irregular Verbs

For one group of irregular verbs, the present, the past, and the past participle are the same.

IRREGULAR VERBS WITH THE SAME PRESENT, PAST, AND PAST PARTICIPLE			
Present	**Present Participle**	**Past**	**Past Participle**
cost	(is) costing	cost	(has) cost
let	(are) letting	let	(have) let
rid	(am) ridding	rid	(have) rid

EXERCISE A: Using Irregular Verbs. Select an irregular verb from the list below to complete each sentence. Be sure to use the correct form.

EXAMPLE: Dad is _____ away the dishes.
Dad is ___*putting*___ away the dishes.

bid	cost	hurt	read
burst	cut	let	rid
cast	hit	put	set

1. The drama teacher has _____ me to play the villain.

2. I am _____ the cheese into slices right now.

3. The child cried in disappointment when his balloon _____.

4. Right now, we are _____ the second chapter.

5. The high jumper _____ his back on the last jump.

6. We have already _____ up the stage.

7. We are _____ John act as the team captain.

8. The Forestry Service has _____ the area of rattle snakes.

9. Is the skateboard _____ you much money?

10. A reckless driver has _____ a parked car.

EXERCISE B. More Work with Irregular Verbs. Complete the sentences below. Use a form of the underlined verb.

EXAMPLE: Are you <u>cutting</u> the grass as I asked?
I already ___*cut*___ the grass.

1. Is this house <u>rid</u> of fleas?

   Yes, our company guarantees it. This house is _____ of fleas!

2. Does your throat <u>hurt</u> anymore?

   It _____ yesterday, but not today.

3. Are you _____ up the chess pieces.

   I have already <u>set</u> them up.

4. I am _____ up the vegetables for the salad.

   Would you <u>cut</u> some of them for me?

5. I <u>let</u> you use the car yesterday.

   Why am I _____ you use it again today?

19.4 Other Irregular Verbs

Some irregular verbs make many changes in spelling as they form the tenses. In some cases, all the principal parts of the verb undergo vowel or consonant changes. The chart below shows several of these irregular verbs. If you are ever confused about an irregular verb, check the dictionary.

IRREGULAR VERBS THAT CHANGE IN A VARIETY OF WAYS			
Present	**Present Participle**	**Past**	**Past Participle**
be	(am) being	was	(have) been
choose	(am) choosing	chose	(have) chosen
ring	(am) ringing	rang	(have) rung
write	(am) writing	wrote	(have) written

EXERCISE A: Completing the Principal Parts of Irregular Verbs. Write the missing parts for the following irregular verbs. Try not to look back at the charts in the text.

EXAMPLE: sing   (am) _____   sang   (have) _____
                sing   (am) _*singing*_   sang   (have) _*sung*_

1. eat   (am) _____   _____   (have) eaten

2. _____   (am) throwing   threw   (have) _____

3. speak   (am) speaking   _____   (have) _____

4. begin   (am) _____   began   (have) _____

5. _____   (am) _____   did   (have) done

6. know   (am) _____   _____   (have) known

7. _____   (am) being   _____   (have) been

8. drink   (am) drinking   _____   (have) _____

9. _____   (am) _____   tore   (have) torn

10. _____   (am) lying   lay   (have) _____

EXERCISE B: Selecting the Correct Forms of Irregular Verbs. Circle the correct form of the verbs given in parentheses in order to complete the sentence.

EXAMPLE: I (drinked, (drank)) too much pool water.

1. You just (tore, tear) your shirt.
2. The choir (sung, sang) the national anthem for us.
3. Are you (thrown, throwing) good curve balls consistently now?
4. Yesterday we (lie, lay) in the sun for a couple of hours.
5. Our family has (driven, drove) across the country on vacation.
6. My brother (swam, swum) underwater for three pool lengths.
7. The manager has (began, begun) to give me more responsibility.
8. I am (doing, done) a report on the Aztec Indians.
9. The fisherman have (rose, risen) early every morning.
10. The winners of the contest are (flying, flew) to the Bahamas.

20.1 The Present, Past, and Future Tenses

Verbs not only describe actions. They can also tell when those actions occur. They do this by changing their form or tense. All the tenses are formed using the four principal parts of a verb.

PRINCIPAL PARTS OF A REGULAR AND IRREGULAR VERB			
Present	**Present Participle**	**Past**	**Past Participle**
live	(am) living	lived	(have) lived
speak	(am) speaking	spoke	(have) spoken

When these parts are combined with different pronouns, we can see all of the forms that a verb can take in a particular tense. This is a verb conjugation.

CONJUGATION OF THE PRESENT, PAST, AND FUTURE TENSES OF TWO VERBS		
	Singular	**Plural**
Present	I live, speak you live, speak he, she, it lives, speaks	we live, speak you live, speak they live, speak
Past	I lived, spoke you lived, spoke he, she, it lived, spoke	we lived, spoke you lived, spoke they lived, spoke
Future	I will live, speak you will live, speak he, she, it will live, speak	we will live, speak you will live, speak they will live, speak

EXERCISE A: Identifying the Present, Past, and Future Verb Tenses. In the blank, write *present, past,* or *future* to identify the verb underlined in each sentence.

EXAMPLE: Nat <u>complained</u> about the heat. __*past*__

1. Banks <u>offer</u> many services. _____

2. The truck <u>drove</u> over the speed limit. _____

3. I <u>will report</u> on precipitation. _____

4. The waiter <u>handed</u> us the check. _____

5. The wind <u>causes</u> the temperature to drop. _____

EXERCISE B: Using the Present, Past, and Future Tenses. In the blank, write the tense of the verb indicated in parentheses.

EXAMPLE: The morning bell just (ring-past) __*rang*__

1. I (do-present) my homework right after school. _____

2. The car (hit-past) only the rear wheel of my bike. _____

3. I (stay-future) here until you return. _____

4. Nancy (lead-past) the group on the hike. _____

5. The band (sing-future) in a benefit performance. _____

6. My mother (water-present) the plants everyday. _____

7. Laurie (keep-present) her purse in her backpack. _____

8. Sally (buy-future) the refreshments. _____

9. The back wheels of the car (stick-past) in the mud. _____

10. Jim (deliver-present) the evening newspaper. _____

20.2 The Present Perfect Tense

The present perfect tense describes an action that always begins in the past. Sometimes, the action also ends in the past, but it may continue into the present. The present perfect tense is formed by using the helping verbs *have* or *has* with the past participle.

<table>
<tr><td colspan="3" align="center">THE PRESENT PERFECT TENSE OF A REGULAR AND
IRREGULAR VERB</td></tr>
<tr><td></td><td>Singular</td><td>Plural</td></tr>
<tr><td>search</td><td>I have searched
you have searched
he, she, it has searched</td><td>we have searched
you have searched
they have searched</td></tr>
<tr><td>win</td><td>I have won
you have won
he, she, it has won</td><td>we have won
you have won
they have won</td></tr>
</table>

EXERCISE A: Using the Present Perfect Tense. In the blank, write the present perfect tense for the underlined verb in each sentence.

EXAMPLE: I walk over twenty miles in two days. ___*have walked*___

1. He throw some fine curve balls. _____

2. The eagle catch his dinner. _____

3. The wood crack from lack of care. _____

4. Sandra give clear directions to her house. _____

5. Our turkey cook for six hours already. _____

6. The jellyfish in this area sting several swimmers. _____

7. Our team win the league championship. _____

8. We observe the stars through our telescope. _____

9. They go outdoors. _____

10. The package arrive. _____

EXERCISE B: More Work with the Present Perfect Tense. Put the verb given into the present perfect tense and use it in a short sentence.

EXAMPLE: refuse
They ___*have refused*___ my help.

1. receive

_____

2. behave

_____

3. lose

_____

4. fly

_____

5. read

_____

20.3 The Present and Past Progressive

Two tenses show continuing action. They are the present progressive and the past progressive. The present progressive is formed by combining the present tense of the helping verb *be* with the present participle.

PRESENT PROGRESSIVE TENSE OF A REGULAR AND AN IRREGULAR VERB	
Singular	**Plural**
I am talking, pay you are talking, paying he, she it is talking, paying	we are talking, paying you are talking, paying they are talking, paying

The past progressive combines the past tense of the helping verb *be* with the present participle.

PAST PROGRESSIVE OF A REGULAR AND AN IRREGULAR VERB	
Singular	**Plural**
I was talking, paying you were talking, paying he, she, it was talking, paying	we were talking, paying you were talking, paying they were talking, paying

EXERCISE A: Identifying the Present Progressive and Past Progressive Tenses. Identify the underlined verb in each sentence. Write *present pro.* if it is the present progressive and *past pro.* if it is past progressive.

EXAMPLE: We <u>were wearing</u> Halloween costumes. ___*past pro.*___

1. I <u>am holding</u> a fortune in my hands. _____

2. We <u>were leading</u> the other teams. _____

3. The Great Dane <u>was chasing</u> a cat. _____

4. The artificial heart <u>is pumping</u> the blood well. _____

5. They <u>were making</u> oatmeal cookies. _____

EXERCISE B: Using the Present Progressive and the Past Progressive. In each blank, write the verb in parentheses, putting it into the tense listed.

EXAMPLE: She (learn-present progressive) U.S. history. ___*is learning*___

1. You (build-present progressive) a strong future. _____

2. The crowd (laugh-past progressive) at the comedian. _____

3. The dock (rise-present progressive) with the tide. _____

4. The elephant (swing-past progressive) his long trunk. _____

5. We (play-past progressive) some soccer. _____

6. I (introduce-present progressive) the speakers. _____

7. They (wrap-present progressive) the packages. _____

8. The farmer (plow-past progressive) his fields today. _____

9. We (rescue-present progressive) stranded animals. _____

10. Chris (pay-present progressive) the bill. _____

21.1 Did and Done

One troublesome verb is *do*. Many people are confused about when to use *did* and *done*. It helps to first memorize the principal parts of the verb *do*.

PRINCIPAL PARTS OF *DO*			
Present	**Present Participle**	**Past**	**Past Participle**
do	(am) doing	did	(have) done

Did is never used with a helping verb, but a helping verb must always accompany *done*.

INCORRECT AND CORRECT USAGE OF *DO*	
Incorrect	**Correct**
They *have did* their homework.	They *did* their homework.
I *done* my research.	I *have done* my research.

EXERCISE A: Using *Did* and *Done*. Circle the correct verb from the two given in parentheses.

EXAMPLE: The crickets have (done, did) damage to the crops.

1. We (done, did) a good day's work.
2. Mary has (done, did) papier-mâché projects before this.
3. The class has (done, did) nothing to celebrate Valentine's Day.
4. I (done, did) my paper route in half the time today.
5. The helmet has (done, did) a good job protecting the rider's head.
6. Exercise has (done, did) me a world of good.
7. Melanie has already (done, did) the decorations.
8. Mother (done, did) her shopping at Roger Wilco.
9. We (done, did) the assignment without any help.
10. You have (done, did) a kind act.

EXERCISE B: More Work with *Did* and *Done*. Correct the sentence by correcting the use of *did* and *done*.

EXAMPLE: I <u>done</u> cake decorating before. ___*have done*___

1. We have <u>did</u> the yardwork for our neighbor. _____
2. May always <u>done</u> the lead in our plays. _____
3. I <u>done</u> the dusting earlier today. _____
4. The loose gravel has <u>did</u> damage to the car's paint. _____
5. The horse <u>done</u> the track in record time. _____

21.2 Lay and Lie

Two verbs that are very different but often confused are *lay* and *lie*. First, they have different meanings. To *lay* means "to put or place something." To *lie* means "to rest in a reclining position" or "to be situated." Second, their principal parts are different.

	Present	Present Participle	Past	Past Participle
PRINICIPAL PARTS OF *LAY* AND *LIE*				
lay	lay	(am) laying	laid	(have) laid
lie	lie	(am) lying	lay	(have) lain

Finally *lay* always takes a direct object while *lie* does not.

EXAMPLES: I *laid* the book on the table.
               I *lay* down for a rest.

EXERCISE A: Using *Lay* and *Lie*. Circle the correct verb from the two given in parentheses.

EXAMPLE: The contractor is (laying, lying) bricks.

1. I have (laid, lain) the rumor to trest.
2. The house (lays, lies) just west of the ridge.
3. We (laid, lay) our picnic basket on the ground.
4. Matt (laid, lay) on the grass, looking up at the clouds.
5. The chickens are (laying, lying) plenty of eggs every day.
6. The kittens (lay, lie) cozily next to their mother.
7. The team's best hope (lays, lies) with the next batter.
8. We have (laid, lain) out the pictures we like best.
9. Tara (laid, lay) on a metal table to have the X-ray taken.
10. The broken tracks are (laying, lying) a mile outside the train station.

EXERCISE B: More Work with *Lay* and *Lie*. Correct each of the underlined verbs by writing in the correct use of *lay* or *lie*.

EXAMPLE: We have <u>lain</u> our bow and arrows down. ___*laid*___

1. The lost doll <u>laid</u> in the dust. _____
2. The fallen trees are <u>laying</u> side by side. _____
3. The dentist <u>lay</u> out the tools he would need. _____
4. Our family <u>lies</u> the presents under the tree. _____
5. The coyote <u>laid</u> in wait for his prey. _____
6. The creek <u>lays</u> between those two mountains. _____
7. She has <u>lain</u> her head on the pillow. _____
8. The pencil is <u>laying</u> next to the phone. _____
9. Yesterday, I <u>lay</u> some carpet. _____
10. Our house is <u>laying</u> southeast of the river. _____

21.3 Set and Sit

Set and *sit* are often confused because they look and sound alike. To tell the difference between the two, remember that *set* means "to put something in place" while *sit* means "to be seated" or "to rest."

PRINCIPAL PARTS OF *SET* AND *SIT*			
Present	Present Participle	Past	Past Participle
set	(am) setting	set	(have) set
sit	(am) sitting	sat	(have) sat

Set is always followed by a direct object. *Sit* is not.

EXAMPLES: I *set* the table.
I *sat* in the easy chair.

EXERCISE A: Using *Set* and *Sit* Correctly. Circle the correct verb of the two shown in parentheses.

EXAMPLE: We (set, sat) near the phone, waiting for the call.

1. The teacher (set, sat) her briefcase down.
2. The troublemakers are (setting, sitting) near the back.
3. I (set, sat) my purse on the table.
4. The clerk is (setting, sitting) the grocery bags in the cart.
5. I (set, sat) next to an air conditioner.
6. The audience has (set, sat) patiently, waiting for the show to start.
7. The photograph is (setting, sitting) on my dresser.
8. Our teacher clearly (set, sat) the standards for the class.
9. Each week Don is (setting, sitting) new school records in track.
10. I (set, sat) beside the lake with my line dangling in the water.

EXERCISE B: More Work with *Set* and *Sit*. Correct each of the underlined verbs by writing in the blank the correct form of *set* or *sat*.

EXAMPLE: I <u>set</u> next to my grandparents. ___*sat*___

1. My dog always <u>sets</u> in my father's favorite chair. _____
2. I <u>sat</u> the lumber down with a thud. _____
3. We have <u>set</u> here all morning. _____
4. Allison <u>sits</u> the dishes in the cupboard. _____
5. I am <u>sitting</u> a good example for my brother. _____
6. The empty garbage cans are <u>setting</u> near the road. _____
7. The waiter <u>sat</u> the bill beside my plate. _____
8. The saddle is <u>setting</u> in the stable. _____
9. Damon has <u>sat</u> our report on the teacher's desk. _____
10. The cast <u>sits</u> the scenery up before the show. _____

22.1 Subject Pronouns

Pronouns used as the subject of a sentence are called subject pronouns.

SUBJECT PRONOUNS
Singular: I, you, he, she, it
Plural: we, you, they

To help you decide on the correct subject pronoun to use, take out any other subjects in a sentence. Then, try saying the sentence with each of the pronouns you are considering; use the one that sounds right.

EXERCISE A: Identifying the Correct Subject Pronoun. Circle the correct subject pronoun from the two in parentheses.

EXAMPLE: Natalie and (I, me) are nominees for class president.

1. Did you or (I, me) volunteer to pick up the food?
2. You and (me, I) can watch television.
3. The Boy Scouts and (us, we) are good campers.
4. Either you or (they, them) will make the decision.
5. Did Lisa and (her, she) stop by your house?
6. Neither (we, us) nor the Red Cross can provide enough medical supplies.
7. My mother and (me, I) are about the same size.
8. Either the fire department or (they, them) should be called.
9. (She, her) and I will miss each other.
10. Has Mark or (he, him) passed the finish line yet?

EXERCISE B: Using the Correct Subject Pronoun. An incorrect pronoun has been used in each sentence. Write in the correct subject pronoun in the blank.

EXAMPLE: My brother and me went to the zoo. ___*I*___

1. We and them will battle for the trophy. _____
2. Neither you nor her has been elected. _____
3. Bill and me collect baseball cards. _____
4. Either they or us will get the new equipment. _____
5. Bill and him have gone on a bike ride. _____
6. Miriam and me joined the swim team. _____
7. Niether we nor them know when the parade starts. _____
8. You and him look very much alike. _____
9. Either it broke by itself or him broke it. _____
10. Neither you nor me likes the cake. _____

22.2 Objective Pronouns

Objective pronouns work in three ways in a sentence: as direct objects, indirect objects, and objects of a preposition.

OBJECTIVE PRONOUNS
Singular: me, you, him, her, it
Plural: us, you, them

USES OF THE OBJECTIVE PRONOUNS	
Direct Object	Margaret drew it. ⟶DO
Indirect Object	Margaret drew her the picture. (IO, DO)
Object of a Preposition	Margaret drew with it. (OBJ)

It may be difficult to choose the correct objective pronoun to use when you have a compound object. To help you, take out the other object and try the pronouns you are considering by themselves.

EXERCISE A: Using Objective Pronouns. Circle the correct pronoun from the two given in parentheses. In the blank, tell how it is being used.

EXAMPLE: I gave (she, her) the correct answer. ___indirect object___

1. Bob will sit behind (she, her). _____
2. Our employer gave (we, us) a raise. _____
3. The coach spoke to (he, him). _____
4. The pickup truck carried (we, us) to the lake. _____
5. A snake slithered toward John and (I, me). _____
6. Mr. Danners sold Sarah and (I, me) some skates. _____
7. Our tour group was just ahead of (they, them). _____
8. Mrs. Fowler introduced (she, her) to us. _____
9. Nancy lent my friends and (I, me) a paddle boat. _____
10. I suggested you and (he, him) for the committee. _____

EXERCISE B: More Work with Objective Pronouns. Complete the sentence by writing in the type of objective pronoun given in parentheses.

EXAMPLE: Dirk offered John and (indirect object) a soft drink. ___me___

1. If you need my book, I will get (direct object). _____
2. When I saw Beth, I waved to (object of a preposition.) _____
3. I want Manuel and (direct object) for my assistants. _____
4. Aunt Jane sent Mary and (indirect object) plane tickets. _____
5. On their wedding day, he gave (indirect object) money. _____
6. Do not argue with (object of preposition). _____
7. I will walk behind the senator and (object of a preposition). _____
8. Mother made Dad and (indirect object) some waffles. _____
9. We were so quiet that the deer didn't hear (direct object). _____
10. The train left without (object of a preposition). _____

22.3 Possessive Pronouns

Possessive forms of personal pronouns show ownership. Sometimes, these pronouns come before a noun, as in the sentence "*Her* paper was excellent." Others are used by themselves, as this example shows: "The judges liked *ours*."

POSSESSIVE PRONOUNS			
Used Before Nouns		**Used By Themselves**	
my	its	mine	its
your	our	yours	ours
his	their	his	theirs
her		hers	

Do not use an apostrophe with a possessive pronoun.

EXERCISE A: Using Possessive Pronouns. Insert a possessive pronoun for the blank in each sentence.

EXAMPLE: Your dog dug a hole in ___*our*___ lawn.

1. Your car has four doors, while _____ has two.

2. _____ clock stopped, and I was late for school.

3. We found _____ cat several miles from home.

4. The infant already responds to _____ name.

5. We have our plan, and they have _____ .

6. _____ car ran out of gas on the freeway.

7. Did you use _____ towel?

8. The redwood tree releases _____ seeds in a fire.

9. We lent them our camera. _____ was out of film.

10. Jack gave _____ butterfly collection to the school.

EXERCISE B: Using Possessive Pronouns Correctly. In each sentence, a possessive pronoun is used incorrectly. Write the correct form in the blank.

EXAMPLE: The tree drops it's leaves each fall. ___*its*___

1. Isn't that coat your's? _____

2. You can tell ours'—it's the one with the blue ribbon. _____

3. His' suitcase was stolen. _____

4. The orchard is theirs' but they let us pick the fruit. _____

5. The town got it's name from a nearby river. _____

6. This is my fishing pole; her's is against the fence. _____

7. Mother's fudge is good, but your's is better. _____

8. His' skateboard just broke in half. _____

9. Our house was safe, but their's was flooded. _____

10. The cat sharpened its' claws on a nearby tree. _____

22.4 Using Different Pronoun Forms

There are three cases of personal pronouns: the nominative, objective and possessive cases. Each case functions in different ways in a sentence.

THE THREE CASES OF PERSONAL PRONOUNS AND THEIR FUNCTIONS		
Cases	**Pronoun Forms**	**Uses**
Nominative	I, you, he, she, it, we, they	*Subject:* He umpired the game. *Predicate Pronoun:* The one to ask is he.
Objective	me, you, him, her, it, us, them	*Direct Object:* Jan helped her. *Indirect Object:* Bob gave me a job. *Object of a Preposition:* I called to her.
Possessive	my, mine, you, yours, his, hers, its, our, ours, their, theirs	*To Show Ownership:* The blue binder is mine. Our costumes look great.

EXERCISE A: Identifying Different Pronoun Cases. In the blank, label the underlined personal pronoun as *nominative, objective,* or *possessive.*

EXAMPLE: Danna went to her for advice. ___*objective*___

1. You are holding up traffic. _____

2. Ours is the best school in the district. _____

3. The vacation had its great moments. _____

4. I told her a secret. _____

5. The manager of the store is she. _____

6. Roger asked me. _____

7. My new haircut looks terrible. _____

8. Did they practice this afternoon? _____

9. Mrs. Bunting baked Spencer and me a cake. _____

10. The Hirschels and we will go in one car. _____

EXERCISE B: Using Different Pronoun Cases. Complete each sentence by inserting the pronoun case indicated in parentheses. There may be several pronouns that will work equally well.

EXAMPLE: Martin gave ___*her*___ the keys to the cabin.   objective

1. _____ want some new paperbacks to read.   (nominative)

2. The coach showed _____ a new technique.   (objective)

3. Here are _____ shoes!   (possessive)

4. The dancer to watch is _____.   (nominative)

5. Either our group or _____ will win the spelling bee.   (possessive)

6. I report to _____.   (objective)

7. _____ house has a large front yard.   (possessive)

8. The highway patrol will catch _____.   (objective)

9. Did _____ ask her name?   (nominative)

10. My answer is correct; _____ isn't.   (possessive)

23.1 Subjects and Verbs

One important rule in writing is that singular subjects must be used with a singular verb and plural subjects must be used with plural verbs. In other words, the subject and verb of a sentence must be in agreement.

AGREEMENT OF SUBJECT AND VERB	
Singular	**Plural**
I want a ride.	My friends want a ride.
The church looks lovely.	The churches look lovely.
He plays in a band.	They play in a band.
The man feels healthy.	The men feel healthy.

Most nouns are made plural by adding *-s* or *-es*. This is not the case with plural verbs. The only verb to add an *-s* is the third person singular.

EXERCISE A: Making Subject and Verbs Agree. Circle the word in parentheses that makes the subject and verb of the sentence agree.

EXAMPLE: Taxes ((climb) climbs) higher most of the time.

1. The cake (mix, mixes) looks too thin.
2. Your dog (bark, barks) at night.
3. Milt (like, likes) the high jump.
4. Our (forest, forests) provide a home for many creatures.
5. Usually his movies (get, gets) good reviews.
6. Dachshunds (stand, stands) low to the ground.
7. (He, they) acts like a clown too often.
8. Our neighbor often (borrow, borrows) tools from us.
9. The fresh (cake, cakes) tastes delicious.
10. They (meet, meets) twice a month.

EXERCISE B: More Work with Subject and Verb Agreement. Correct the underlined word in each sentence so that the subject and verb are in agreement.

EXAMPLE: Mary <u>dress</u> fashionably. ___*dresses*___

1. We <u>sees</u> the Golden Gate Bridge. _____
2. <u>Bird</u> fly south for the winter. _____
3. The bed <u>sit</u> below the window. _____
4. <u>They</u> adds the numbers on a calculator. _____
5. The horses' hooves <u>clinks</u> on the road. _____
6. I <u>enters</u> from the left side of the stage. _____
7. <u>We</u> plays in the band. _____
8. My great-grandmother <u>send</u> money on my birthday. _____
9. The <u>kite</u> soar high in the sky. _____
10. The woman <u>weave</u> cloth on a loom. _____

23.2 Compound Subjects and Verbs

When a compound subject is connected by *and*, the verb is usually plural. But when the parts of the compound subject are thought of as one person or thing, the verb is singular.

COMPOUND SUBJECTS JOINED BY *AND*
Shirts and a new tie *are* on my shopping list. Chicken and broccoli *is* a popular Chinese dish.

Two singular subjects joined by *or* or *nor* take a singular verb. Two plural subjects joined by *or* or *nor* take a plural verb. When singular and plural subjects are joined by *or* or *nor*, the verb agrees with the subject closer to it.

COMPOUND SUBJECTS JOINED BY *OR* OR *NOR*
Neither Sue nor Pam *has* her ice skates. Tigers or lions *are* what I went to the zoo to see. The magazines or the book *has* the information you need.

EXERCISE A: Making Compound Subjects and Verbs Agree. Circle the verb that agrees with the subject of each sentence.

EXAMPLE: The parents and children (play, plays) on opposite teams.

1. Black and white (is, are) my favorite color combination.
2. The trees and shrubs (look, looks) nice today.
3. Placemats or a tablecloth (go, goes) in the picnic basket.
4. Trucks and tractors (slow, slows) traffic down.
5. Neither the men nor the women (want, wants) that rule.
6. Either Sally or Eric (bring, brings) the main course.
7. Shirt and tie (look, looks) best at a formal dinner.
8. Either chicken or steak (taste, tastes) good when barbecued.
9. Neither the couch nor the chairs (look, looks) right in the room.
10. Swimming and running (is, are) good ways to exercise.

EXERCISE B. More Work with Compound Subjects and Verbs. Circle the verb that agrees with the subject of each sentence.

EXAMPLE: Canada and the United States (stay, stays) friendly.

1. Neither my coat nor my dresses (is, are) in the suitcase.
2. Dell and Amy really (like, likes) science.
3. The St. Bernard and the terrier (play, plays) together.
4. Either the cheese or the fish (is, are) bad.
5. The eggs and the milk (go, goes) in next.
6. Neither the sheets nor the bedspread (fit, fits) the bed.
7. *Life* and *Monopoly* (is, are) my favorite games.
8. The cows or sheep (move, moves) to another pasture in the afternoon.
9. A salamander or snake (live, lives) under that rock.
10. The coaches and the managers (run, runs) the team.

23.3 Pronoun Subjects and Verbs

An indefinite pronoun used as the subject of a sentence must agree with the verb. Some indefinite pronouns are always singular and therefore take a singular verb. Some are always plural and require a plural verb. For those pronouns that can be either singular or plural, look back at the noun that they replace. If the noun is singular, the pronoun is also singular.

INDEFINITE PRONOUNS				
Singular			**Plural**	**Singular or Plural**
anybody	everyone	nothing	both	all
anyone	everything	one	few	any
anything	much	other	many	more
each	neither	somebody	others	most
either	nobody	someone	several	none
everybody	no one	something		

EXERCISE A: Making Pronoun Subjects and Verbs Agree. Circle the verb that agrees with the pronoun subject.

EXAMPLE: Everybody in the office (know, (knows)) how to type.

1. Few of us (like, likes) Brussels sprouts.
2. All of the work (is, are) ready for you to inspect.
3. Nothing (get, gets) in his way.
4. Each of the stores (contribute, contributes) a gift.
5. Most of my friends (want, wants) to dance.
6. Several of the homes (have, has) fire damage.
7. Nobody (laugh, laughs) at his jokes.
8. None of the equipment (belong, belongs) to me.
9. Many of the teachers (give, gives) homework every night.
10. Each of our pets (try, tries) to please us.

EXERCISE B: More Work With Pronoun Subject and Verb Agreement. After each sentence, the present tense of the verb is given. In the blank, write the form of the verb that agrees with the pronoun subject.

EXAMPLE: Everybody __helps__ with school clean-up. help

1. Most of the newspaper _____ advertisements. be
2. Neither of my younger brothers _____ cartoons. watch
3. Few of the people _____ for the whole day. stay
4. All of the jewelry _____ antique. look
5. Everything in the box _____ to the Goodwill. go
6. Someone _____ that idea every year. suggest
7. Both of my parents _____ the opera. enjoy
8. All of those interested _____ on Tuesday. vote
9. One of my friends _____ a gymnast. be
10. Everyone _____ for a speedy recovery. hope

23.4 Pronouns and Antecedents

A pronoun and its antecedent, or the word that it stands for, must always agree. A singular antecedent takes a singular pronoun. A plural antecedent takes a plural pronoun. If the antecedents are compound, use the following rule: use a singular pronoun when the antecedents are joined by *or* or *nor*, and use a plural pronoun when the antecedents are joined by *and*.

PRONOUNS AND THEIR ANTECEDENTS	
Antecedent	**Example**
Singular	The gentleman said *he* would wait.
Plural	The women called *their* lawyer.
Compound joined by *or* or *nor*.	Neither Mike nor Dick brought *his* lunch money.
Compound joined by *and*.	The parents and children sang *their* favorite songs.

EXERCISE A: Making Pronouns and Antecedents Agree. Fill in the blank with a pronoun that agrees with its antecedent.

EXAMPLE: The cab driver said __*his*__ car needed a tune-up.

1. The custodian took _____ lunch break at noon.

2. Thomas Edison obtained 1,100 patents for _____ inventions.

3. The fire engine had _____ siren blaring.

4. Mary owns one of the hamsters; _____ is the brown one.

5. Gene and Greg gave _____ mother an apron.

6. Dad bakes bread, and _____ is delicious.

7. Either Jack or Brandon gives _____ speech next.

8. The pilots said _____ could fly the new plane.

9. Both the doctor and his assistant gave _____ opinions.

10. John and I wanted to help but _____ offer wasn't in time.

EXERCISE B: More Work with Pronouns and Antecedents. Write *correct* for those sentences containing no pronoun-antecedent errors. Rewrite those sentences with errors, changing the pronouns so that they agree with the antecedent.

EXAMPLE: The men must wear his coats and ties into the restaurant.
      The men must wear their coats and ties into the restaurant.

1. Anne and Bob made her parents a photograph album.

_____

2. My dress does not fit right, so they must be altered.

_____

3. Either Sara or Nicole gives their speech next.

_____

4. My little sister played with its stuffed toy.

_____

5. The members of the team practiced its dribbling.

_____

24.1 Using Adjectives to Compare

Adjectives can compare items. To do this, adjectives have three degrees of comparison: the positive, the comparative, and the superlative. Most one- and two-syllable adjectives form the comparative by adding -er to the end of the word and the superlative by adding -est to the end.

DEGREES OF COMPARISON FORMED BY ADDING -ER AND -EST		
Positive	**Comparative**	**Superlative**
rich	richer	richest
sweet	sweeter	sweetest
tidy	tidier	tidiest

In words ending in -y, like *tidy,* the -y is often changed to -i before adding the -er or -est.

EXERCISE A: Forming Positive, Comparative, and Superlative Adjectives. Fill in the chart below with the missing positive, comparative, and superlative adjectives.

EXAMPLE: crisp   *crisper*   *crispest*

1. _____   paler   _____

2. wild   _____   _____

3. _____   _____   quickest

4. small   _____   _____

5. _____   _____   curliest

6. _____   happier   _____

7. clean   _____   _____

8. _____   _____   dirtiest

9. _____   firmer   _____

10. tall   _____   _____

EXERCISE B: More Work with Positive, Comparative, and Superlative Adjectives. Write a second sentence using the underlined adjective as described.

EXAMPLE: Today the sky is <u>cloudy</u>.
        Comparative: *Today, the sky is cloudier than yesterday.*

1. Am I <u>early</u>?
   Superlative: _____

2. My grandfather is <u>old</u>.
   Comparative: _____

3. This bridge is <u>narrow</u>.
   Comparative: _____

4. The bus driver looks <u>sleepy</u>.
   Comparative: _____

5. The weather is the <u>calmest</u> I have seen it.
   Positive: _____

24.2 Using Adjectives with *More* and *Most*

Another way to form the comparative and superlative of adjectives is to add *more* and *most*. All adjectives over two syllables will use these words to form comparisons. Even some one- and two-syllable adjectives can use them.

SOME MODIFIERS REQUIRING *MORE* AND *MOST*		
Positive	**Comparative**	**Superlative**
delicious	more delicious	most delicious
attractive	more attractive	most attractive
willing	more willing	most willing
alert	more alert	most alert

EXERCISE A: Forming Degrees of Comparison with *More* and *Most*. Fill in the chart below with the degrees of comparison that are missing.

EXAMPLE: pleasing _____*more pleasing*_____ _____*most pleasing*_____

1. _____ more convenient _____

2. _____ _____ most generous

3. _____ more useful _____

4. apparent _____ _____

5. protective _____ _____

6. _____ _____ most unfair

   _____ _____ most outstanding

8. _____ more faithful _____

9. profitable _____ _____

10. _____ more surprising _____

EXERCISE B: More Work with Forming Comparisons Using *More* and *Most*. Use *more* or *most* to form the comparative or superlative form of each adjective shown in parentheses.

EXAMPLE: She was the (disagreeable) girl I ever met. ___*most disagreeable*___

1. Your answer is (reasonable) than the one he gave. _____

2. Smoking is (harmful) to your lungs. _____

3. Are oaks (big) than maple trees? _____

4. This is the (worthwhile) project I have done. _____

5. Silk is (expensive) than cotton. _____

6. That child is (talkative) than the others. _____

7. You are the (considerate) friend I have. _____

8. It is (fortunate) that you arrived now. _____

9. This is a (interesting) letter than your last one. _____

10. This camp has made me (homesick) than I was before. _____

24.3 Using Adverbs to Compare

Adverbs, like adjectives, have three degrees of comparison: the positive, comparative, and superlative. With a one-syllable adverb, the comparative is formed by adding *-er* and the superlative by adding *-est*.

DEGREES OF COMPARISON FORMED BY ADDING -ER OR -EST		
Positive	**Comparative**	**Superlative**
low	lower	lowest
straight	straighter	straightest

Adverbs ending in *-ly* form the two comparisons by adding *more* and *most*.

DEGREES OF COMPARISON FORMED BY ADDING MORE OR MOST		
Positive	**Comparative**	**Superlative**
briefly	more briefly	most briefly
cheerfully	more cheerfully	most cheerfully

EXERCISE A: Forming the Comparative and Superlative Degrees of Adverbs. Fill in the chart with the missing positive, comparative, and superlative degrees of the adverbs.

EXAMPLE: sincerely   *more sincerely*   *most sincerely*

1. _____   more slowly   _____

2. long   _____   _____

3. _____   more quietly   _____

4. _____   _____   most carefully

5. willingly   _____   _____

6. _____   _____   most loudly

7. _____   more easily   _____

8. _____   _____   most recently

9. completely   _____   _____

10. often   _____   _____

EXERCISE B: More Work with Positive, Comparative, and Superlative Adverbs. Write a sentence using the underlined adverb in the form indicated.

EXAMPLE: Matt exercises <u>regularly</u>.
         Comparative: _*Matt exercises more regularly than I do.*_

1. We ride <u>most cautiously</u> on busy streets.

   Positive: _____

2. I behaved <u>selfishly</u>.

   Comparative: _____

3. You spoke <u>bluntly</u>.

   Comparative: _____

4. I hit the nail <u>hard</u>.

   Superlative: _____

25.1 Using *Bad* and *Badly*

Knowing when to use *bad* or *badly* can be a problem. Remember, *bad* is an adjective and describes a noun. It usually follows linking verbs like *be, look, appear, seem, smell, stay,* and *taste*. *Badly* is an adverb and follows an action verb.

USING *BAD* AND *BADLY* IN SENTENCES	
bad	The road to the cabin is *bad*. The fish smells *bad*. My cut looks *bad*.
badly	My sister cleans house *badly*. Today, I swam *badly*. His hands shook *badly*.

EXERCISE A: Using *Bad* and *Badly* Correctly. Circle the correct modifier, *bad* or *badly*, in each sentence below.

EXAMPLE: The rehearsal went (bad, (badly).)

1. Our dog behaves (bad, badly).
2. The smog is (bad, badly) today.
3. The burnt asparagus smells (bad, badly).
4. I draw straight lines (bad, badly).
5. Her science project looks (bad, badly).
6. Mother reacted (bad, badly) to my suggestion.
7. Our lawn mower works (bad, badly).
8. Milk turns (bad, badly) when it isn't refrigerated.
9. My broken arm hurts (bad, badly).
10. The fire seems (bad, badly).

EXERCISE B: More Work with *Bad* and *Badly*. Write in the correct modifier, *bad* or *badly*, for each sentence.

EXAMPLE: The color red looks <u>bad</u> on me.

1. The average score on the test was very _____.
2. The child acts _____ when his parents aren't home.
3. The lawyer wrote the contract _____.
4. Our sailboat handled _____ in the rough water.
5. The results of the hurricane were _____.
6. The speaker's microphone worked _____.
7. The host felt _____ when the guest of honor didn't show up.
8. The foundation under the house was _____.
9. The new plants did _____ in the summer heat.
10. My dog performed _____ in her first dog show.

25.2 Using *Good* and *Well*

Good and *well* often confuse writers. *Good* is an adjective and must always follow a linking verb. *Well* can be either an adverb or adjective. As an adverb, it always follows an action verb. As an adjective, it follows a linking verb and generally refers to a person's health.

EXAMPLES OF *GOOD* AND *WELL*		
Word	**Use**	**Example**
Good	Adjective	The warm water feels *good*. Your homemade bread tastes *good*.
Well	Adverb	I ride a horse *well*. Our candy sold *well*.
Well	Adjective	Your ears look *well* with the infection gone. My grandfather feels *well*.

EXERCISE A: Using *Good* and *Well* Correctly. Circle the correct modifier, *good* or *well*, to complete each sentence.

EXAMPLE: The first leg of the race went (good, (well)).

1. My brand-new bike rides (good, well).
2. The frozen yogurt tasted (good, well).
3. She handled her disappointment (good, well).
4. The last two movies I've seen have been (good, well).
5. Are you feeling (good, well) now that your fever has dropped?
6. The teacher said my report on the Gold Rush was (good, well).
7. My parents dance (good, well) together.
8. I had the flu, but I am (good, well) now.
9. My teen-age brother drives (good, well).
10. A cool breeze feels (good, well) on a hot day.

EXERCISE B: More Practice Using *Good* and *Well*. Insert the correct modifier, *good* or *well*, to complete each sentence.

EXAMPLE: The new engine runs well.

1. The sand feels _____ between my toes.
2. That dress looks _____ on you.
3. You are looking _____ even after running a marathon.
4. Nancy spoke _____ before the large crowd.
5. Despite the insects, the trees still appear _____.
6. This muffin mix stays _____ for several weeks if refrigerated.
7. These lightweight shoes are _____ for backpacking.
8. I feel _____ enough to be out of bed.
9. The students reacted _____ when the fire alarm went off.
10. The first act of the play was very _____.

26.1 Avoiding Double Comparisons

If two forms of comparison—for instance, *most* and *-est*—are used in one sentence, it results in a sentence error called a double comparison. To avoid the error, use either *-er* or *more* to form the comparative and *-est* or *most* to form the superlative. Never use both in the same comparison.

CORRECTING DOUBLE COMPARISONS	
Incorrect	**Correct**
I ran *more faster* today than yesterday.	I ran *faster* today than yesterday.
A plum is *more sweeter* than a pear.	A plum is *more sweet* than a pear.
This is the *most cleanest* room.	This is the *cleanest* room.
She worked the *most hardest* of all.	She worked the *hardest* of all.

EXERCISE A: Avoiding Double Comparisons. Rewrite the underlined part of each sentence to get rid of the double comparison.

EXAMPLE: I felt *more happier* after I heard the news. ____*happier*____

1. These are the most crispest potato chips. _____

2. I have more curlier hair than my sister. _____

3. Fudge tastes the most richest of all candy. _____

4. The crew made the road more wider. _____

5. I promise to call more oftener. _____

6. This cartoon ran the most longest. _____

7. The wood is the most hardest you can buy. _____

8. The music is more louder than I like. _____

9. My dog is the most gentlest on the block. _____

10. I look the most sleepiest in the morning. _____

EXERCISE B: More Work Correcting Double Comparisons. Rewrite the underlined portion of each sentence to get rid of the double comparison.

EXAMPLE: My grandmother is the most oldest member of her family. ____*oldest*____

1. This test seemed more shorter than the last. _____

2. I am the most handiest at fixing cars. _____

3. That author wrote the most dullest book. _____

4. The kitten grew more bigger each day. _____

5. This grocery store sells meat the most cheapest. _____

6. I can't remember when I've felt more worser. _____

7. The rain fell the most hardest in the valley. _____

8. My brother is the most stubbornest boy around. _____

9. We arrived more later than we thought. _____

10. Our dog obeyed us more better after obedience school. _____

26.2 Avoiding Double Negatives

Only one negative word is needed to give a sentence a negative meaning. Putting in more than this is a sentence error called a double negative.

NEGATIVE WORDS				
never	nobody	no one	not	nowhere
no	none	nor	nothing	n't

To correct a double negative, remove one of the negative words or change one to a positive.

CORRECTING DOUBLE NEGATIVES	
Double Negative	**Corrected Sentence**
We *can't* let *nobody* know about it.	We *can't* let *anybody* know about it. We *can* let *nobody* know about it.
I *can't* find the cat *nowhere*.	I *can't* find the cat *anywhere*. I *can* find the cat *nowhere*.

EXERCISE A: Correcting Double Negatives. Circle the word in parentheses that makes each sentence negative without creating a double negative.

EXAMPLE: I wouldn't have (none, (any)) of the spinach.

1. Our family never does (nothing, anything) on the weekends.
2. The manager (can, can't) seem to keep nobody working for him.
3. I wouldn't have (no, any) part in playing that trick on Rod.
4. Those books (are, aren't) none of mine.
5. I never go (nowhere, anywhere) without buckling my seatbelt.

EXERCISE B: More Work Correcting Sentences with Double Negatives. Correct each sentence by getting rid of the double negative in two ways.

EXAMPLE: I haven't never heard of that brand of ice cream.
  I haven't ever heard of that brand of ice cream.
  I have never heard of that brand of ice cream.

1. Max shouldn't never have tried to fix it himself.

_____

_____

2. We haven't heard nothing about your trip to Canada.

_____

_____

3. Your keys weren't nowhere that I could see.

_____

_____

4. My father says I never hear nothing that he says.

_____

_____

5. I didn't want help from nobody.

_____

_____

NAME _____ CLASS _____ DATE _____

27.1 Capitals for Sentences and the Word *I*

Capital letters signal the start of sentences and important words. A capital always begins the first word of a sentence whether it is a statement, question, or direct quotation. Also the word *I* is always capitalized.

CAPITALS USED WITH SENTENCES AND THE WORD *I*	
Always Capitalize:	**Examples**
the first word in a sentence	*R*accoons got into the trash last night. *W*here will the signal come from?
the first word in a direct quotation	Mike said, "*T*he lawn needs water." "*I*f I do it," Jan said, "will you pay me?"
the word *I*	*I* wondered if *I* had enough time.

EXERCISE A: Using Capitals to Begin Sentences. Underline the word or words that should be capitalized in each sentence.

EXAMPLE: <u>the</u> boys asked, "<u>can</u> we go to the movies?"

1. when i was younger, i took lessons on the clarinet.
2. clipper ships were built with tall masts and sharp lines.
3. "crocodile hide," our teacher said, "is sometimes made into leather."
4. she asked, "does the recipe call for brown sugar?"
5. i will do it only if i have the proper safety equipment.
6. my mother asked, "can you help me vacuum the family room?"
7. the reporter noted, "killer bees have been found in the United States."
8. i have several valuable stamps in a collection i started last year.
9. "when i was a boy," my grandfather recalled, "i loved to play leapfrog."
10. our speaker said, "a nutritious diet is important to your health."

EXERCISE B: More Work with Capital Letters. Complete each blank with an appropriate word or words. Capitalize the word if necessary.

EXAMPLE: Mother said, ___"Bread"___ is on sale at the market."

1. _____ wants to go to the beach with us.
2. Mother asked, "_____ should I serve dinner?"
3. You can get Vitamin C from _____.
4. I said, "_____ is my favorite food."
5. Either _____ go or you go, but we can't both go.
6. "_____ topic have you chosen for your report?" the teacher asked.
7. _____ told her, "_____ can't decide on a subject."
8. Our _____ broke down and had to be repaired.
9. "On Halloween," Nan said, "_____ start trick-or-treating about seven."
10. _____ are a fast form of transportation.

78 Copyright © by Prentice-Hall, Inc.

27.2 Capitals for Names of People and Places

When naming a *specific* person or place, capital letters should be used.

CAPITALS FOR SPECIFIC NAMES AND PLACES	
Persons	Louisa May Alcott, J. Edgar Hoover, Mickey Mouse
Streets and Roads	Mill Road, Washington Avenue, Fifth Street
Cities and States	Santa Fe, Chicago, Paris, Wisconsin, Oregon
Nations and Continents	Egypt, Finland, Australia, South America
Land Forms	Mount Shasta, the Central Valley, Virgin Islands, the Mojave Desert
Bodies of Water	Gold Lake, Hudson Bay, Arabian Sea, Yukon River, the Pacific Ocean.

EXERCISE A: Using Capital Letters with Specific People and Places. Underline each letter that should be capitalized.

EXAMPLE: hank aaron hit 755 home runs in his career.

1. britain fought a war over the falkland islands.
2. The lowest point below sea level is found in death valley, california.
3. robert e. peary was the first person to reach the north pole.
4. Many animal studies are done on the galápagos islands in ecuador.
5. john f. kennedy defeated richard m. nixon in a close election in 1960.
6. The arabian desert is over 70,000 square miles in size.
7. The President of the united states lives on pennsylvania avenue.
8. The sacramento river empties into the san francisco bay.
9. The most recent eruption of mount st. helens in washington was 1984.
10. The mysterious Bermuda Triangle is found in the atlantic ocean.

EXERCISE B: More Work with Capitalizing Specific Names and Places. Fill in each blank with an appropriate word or words. Capitalize when necessary.

EXAMPLE: I once took a boat to __Catalina Island.__

1. The ocean nearest my home is _____.
2. My address is _____.
3. My grandfather's full name is _____.
4. I have visited these states: _____.
5. I would like to travel to the country of _____.
6. The closest mountains to my home are _____.
7. It would be fun to go fishing in the _____ River.
8. Canada is located on the _____ continent.
9. Italy is near the _____ Sea.
10. The most famous city near my home is _____.

27.3 Capitals for Names of Specific Things

The names of *specific* things—such as special days, events, or objects—should always be capitalized.

CAPITALS FOR SPECIFIC THINGS	
Historical Periods, Events, and Documents	Industrial Revolution, Civil War, Declaration of Independence
Days, Months, and Holidays	Saturday, October, Thanksgiving
Organizations and Schools	Girl Scouts, Miller Elementary School
Government Bodies and Political Parties	the Congress, the Republican Party
Races, Nationalities, and Languages	Eskimo, Chinese, French
Monuments, Memorials, and Buildings	Statue of Liberty, the Vietnam Memorial, the Eiffel Tower
Religious Faiths	Judaism, Christianity, Hinduism
Awards	Oscars, Caldecott Medal
Air, Sea, Space, and Land Craft	*Double Eagle II, Lusitania, Skylab 2, Mustang*

EXERCISE A: Using Capitals for the Names of Specific Things. Underline the letters of words requiring capitals in the sentences below.

EXAMPLE: The liberty bell was cracked in september of 1752.

1. Four presidents are sculptured in the monument at mount rushmore.
2. One new form of mass transit is the system called amtrak.
3. memorial day is usually celebrated on the last monday in may.
4. Most people in turkey are muslims.
5. In somalia, the official languages are somali and arabic.
6. The concorde flew from New York to Paris in 3 hours 30 minutes.
7. The tallest building in the world is the sears tower in Chicago.
8. The symbol for the democratic party is the donkey.
9. Satellites have been launched from the space shuttle *challenger*.
10. A woman is now a member of the supreme court.

EXERCISE B: More Work Capitalizing Specific Things. In each pair, one item is general and one is specific. Underline the letters in the specific item that need capitalizing.

EXAMPLE: a lawyer's contract   the equal rights amendment

1.	a single-engine plane	the spirit of st. louis
2.	the medal of honor	an achievement award
3.	a conservative group	the republican party
4.	our elected group	the congress
5.	father's day	a day for fathers
6.	bill of rights	a list of guaranteed rights
7.	a church group	christians
8.	the sewing group	national sewing association
9.	the model t	an old car
10.	june	the month for weddings

27.4 Capitals for Titles of People

There are three kinds of titles: social, professional, and family titles. Generally, you capitalize these titles when they come before a person's name or in direct address. You also capitalize a family title when it refers to a specific person but does not follow a possessive noun or possessive pronoun.

CAPITALS WITH SOCIAL, PROFESSIONAL, AND FAMILY TITLES		
Title	Examples	Use in a Sentence
Social	Miss, Madame, Mister, Sir, Mesdames	Could you help me, *Sir*? Our guest is *Mr*. David Gatley. I seated the *mesdames* at that table.
Professional	Senator, Mayor, Judge, Doctor, Sergeant, Rabbi, Sister, Professor	The service was led by *Father* John. Did the men finish the drill, *Corporal*? The *doctor* cured the man.
Family	Mother, Father, Aunt, Uncle, Grandmother, Grandfather	I love *Uncle John's* farm. Is this the picture you meant, *Mother*? Your *father* will be able to fix it.

EXERCISE A: Capitalizing Titles of People. Underline each title that requires capitalization. Some sentences may have no titles requiring capitalization.

EXAMPLE: Ask <u>sister</u> Joan to come to the chapel.

1. Can you tell us, congresswoman Filante, how you will vote on the issue?
2. The doctor is at lunch right now.
3. I understand judge Canyon will hear the case.
4. Was that lieutenant Randolph who just walked by?
5. Who is your favorite French author, professor?

EXERCISE B: More Work Capitalizing Titles of People. Use each title given in two ways—first, where it requires a capital and, second, where it does not.

EXAMPLE: private
   I am Private Thomas Jackson reporting for duty.
   That private wears his uniform with pride.

1. uncle

2. governor

3. attorney

4. doctor

5. mother

27.5 Capitals for Titles of Things

Capitals are used with the titles of written works and works of art. You should capitalize the first word and all other key words in these titles. The title of a school course is capitalized only when it is followed by a number or refers to a language.

TITLES OF WRITTEN WORKS, WORKS OF ART, AND SCHOOL COURSES	
Books	*Swiss Family Robinson, Kontiki*
Newspapers and Magazines	*The Daily Journal, Outdoor Life*
Short Stories and Poems	"The Loser," "Richard Cory"
Full-length Plays	*Cats, The Music Man*
Movies	*Raiders of the Lost Ark, Star Wars*
Songs	"Hello Dolly," "Puttin' on the Ritz"
Paintings and Sculptures	*Young Woman with a Water Jug, Boxing Match*
School Courses	English 2A, German, Science I

EXERCISE A: Using Capitals for Titles of Things. Circle the letters in the titles that require capital letters.

EXAMPLE: *the enchanted castle*—painting

1. *splash*—movie
2. *reader's digest*—magazine
3. *the sign of the beaver*—book
4. spanish—school course
5. orlando *sentinel*—newspaper
6. "you've got a friend"—song
7. *fiddler on the roof*—play
8. *the thinker*—sculpture
9. *jane eyre*—book
10. "the bridge"—poem
11. *the peasant dance*—painting
12. composition 2—school course
13. "ol' man river"—song
14. *chariots of fire*—movie
15. tucson *daily star*—newspaper
16. *life*—magazine
17. *the cat in the hat*—book
18. *haystacks*—painting
19. *our town*—play
20. "trees"—poem

EXERCISE B: More Work With Capitalizing Titles of Things. Circle any letters in the titles that need capitalizing in the sentences below.

EXAMPLE: The poem "annabel lee" was written about Poe's wife.

1. *through the looking glass,* by Lewis Carroll, has become a classic book.
2. I try to read the denver *post* in the bus on the way to work.
3. The longest running play in the United States is *chorus line*.
4. My counselor signed me up for english I next year.
5. I enjoyed reading *that was then, this is now.*
6. Puppets were used in the movie *the muppets take manhattan.*
7. My brother has taken both french and latin in high school.
8. *sports afield* is a magazine for people who enjoy hunting.
9. One of Michael Jackson's gold records is "the girl is mine."
10. Thomas Gainsborough painted *the blue boy.*

27.6 Capitals in Letters

Friendly letters require capital letters in several places—the heading, the salutation, and the closing.

CAPITALS IN FRIENDLY LETTERS		
Heading	14 Carolyn Drive Newark, New Jersey 07102 August 2, 1985	
Salutations	Dear Ellen, Dear Mr. Rodgers,	My dear Family, Dear Aunt Harriet,
Closings	Always, Your friend,	Fondly, With love,

EXERCISE A: Using Capitals in Letters. Underline the words that need capitals in the parts of letters below.

EXAMPLE: <u>with</u> fond regards,

1. my dear sister,
2. 410 camilia lane
   new orleans, louisiana 70130
   april 17, 1985
3. your good friend,
4. dear mrs. dunkin,
5. 1620 vineyard avenue
   baltimore, maryland 21202
   february 14, 1988

6. affectionately,
7. dear grandma ethel,
8. my dear mr. larusso,
9. 1213 dunning way
   akron, ohio 44308
   january 1, 1986
10. 16 sunset lane
   fort wayne, indiana 46802
   november 23, 1988

EXERCISE B: More Practice in Using Capitals in Letters. Give the information requested, using capitals where necessary.

EXAMPLE: Write a closing for a letter to a friend.
     Thinking of you,

1. Write your address and today's date as it would look in a letter heading.

   _____

   _____

2. Write the closing you would use in a letter to your parents.

   _____

3. Write the salutation you would use in a letter to an adult neighbor.

   _____

4. Write the salutation you would use in a letter to an aunt or uncle.

   _____

5. Write the closing you would use in a letter to a friend in class.

   _____

28.1 Abbreviations for Titles of People

When using a social or professional title of a person, an abbreviation is often used. These abbreviations should begin with a capital letter and end with a period.

ABBREVIATIONS OF SOCIAL AND PROFESSIONAL TITLES	
Social	Singular: Mr. Davis Mrs. Barnet Mme. Lemand Plural: Messrs. Donner and Wilson Mmes. Hall and Decker Note: Ms., Miss, and Misses are titles, but not abbreviations.
Governmental	Rep. (Representative) Gov. (Governor) Sen. (Senator) Treas. (Treasurer) Sec. (Secretary) Pres. (President)
Military	Pvt. (Private) Corp. (Corporal) Lt. (Lieutenant) Maj. (Major) Gen. (General) Sgt. (Sergeant)
Professional	Dr. (Doctor) Atty. (Attorney) Prof. (Professor) Rev. (Reverend) Sr. (Sister) Hon. (Honorable)

EXERCISE A: Using Abbreviations for Titles of People. In the blank write the abbreviation for the title used in the sentence.

EXAMPLE: ___Sec.___ You have an appointment with Secretary Nelson today.

_____ 1. Corporal Max Klinger was a character on *M.A.S.H.*

_____ 2. A new article was published by Professor Ann Danforth.

_____ 3. I have a package for Senator Brent Jarcik.

_____ 4. Do we have Mister Zak Arnold's address in our file?

_____ 5. A grant was awarded to Doctor Halpin.

_____ 6. The medal goes to Sergeant Phyllis Brown.

_____ 7. I think Madames Jane Brandon and Doris Dahl have arrived.

_____ 8. Governor James Norton has vetoed several bills.

_____ 9. We will have Reverend Donald Thomas do our wedding.

_____ 10. Treasurer Jean Bowman has our books balanced.

EXERCISE B: More Practice Abbreviating Titles of People. Next to each item, write the correct abbreviation for the title and the person's name.

EXAMPLE: Senator in your state: ___Sen. John Jeremiah___

1. Your doctor's name: _____

2. The governor in your state: _____

3. Your mother's name: _____

4. The President of the United States: _____

5. A title you might have if you were in the military: _____

28.2 Abbreviations for Names of Places

Abbreviations for the names of places are saved for use in informal writing. When an abbreviation for the name of a place comes before or after a proper noun, it should begin with a capital letter and end with a period.

ABBREVIATIONS FOR COMMON PLACE NAMES					
Ave.	Avenue	Hwy.	Highway	Rd.	Road
Bldg.	Building	Is.	Island	Rte.	Route
Blvd.	Boulevard	Jct.	Junction	Sq.	Square
Co.	County	Mt.	Mountain	St.	Street
Ct.	Court	Pen.	Peninsula	Ter.	Terrace
Dr.	Drive	Pk.	Park, Peak	Tpk.	Turnpike
Ft.	Fort	Pl.	Place		

EXERCISE A: Using Abbreviations for the Names of Places. In the blank, write the abbreviation for the underlined word in each sentence.

EXAMPLE: _____Co.____ I was born in Apache <u>County</u> in Arizona.

_____ 1. The Tamalpais State <u>Park</u> was closed for two weeks.

_____ 2. Our relatives live on <u>Route</u> 17 in Nebraska.

_____ 3. We visited <u>Mountain</u> Rainier in Washington.

_____ 4. Our cruise did not go to Martinique <u>Island</u>.

_____ 5. I saw some construction out on Wilson <u>Drive</u>.

_____ 6. Plans call for widening <u>Highway</u> 101 next year.

_____ 7. Their office is located in the Stratford <u>Building</u>.

_____ 8. Let's meet at Trenton <u>Square</u>, off Handel Avenue.

_____ 9. The Monterrey <u>Peninsula</u> is a lovely vacation spot.

_____ 10. <u>Fort</u> Ross is where the Russians first landed in the United States.

EXERCISE B: More Work with Abbreviating the Names of Places. Write out the full word for the abbreviation used in each sentence.

EXAMPLE: _____drive____ The car is at the corner of Center Dr. and Sutro Avenue.

_____ 1. Many lovely crafts can be found in the Blue Ridge Mts.

_____ 2. My address is 27 McClay Rd.

_____ 3. The sign read "The World's Most Scenic Hwy."

_____ 4. Protestors gathered in London's Trafalgar Sq.

_____ 5. From Jackson Pk. you have a view of the entire valley.

_____ 6. We drove past Atherton Pl. before turning left.

_____ 7. The rides are great at Coney Is.

_____ 8. The road was named Blvd. of Kings.

_____ 9. We took the Oklahoma City Tkp. for the first time.

_____ 10. I used to catch frogs at Steven's Creek Pk.

28.3 Abbreviations for Names of States

When writing the name of a state on an envelope, Postal Service abbreviations should be used. Both letters in these abbreviations are capitalized and no period follows the abbreviation.

POSTAL SERVICE ABBREVIATIONS FOR NAMES OF STATES		
AL Alabama	LA Louisiana	OH Ohio
AK Alaska	ME Maine	OK Oklahoma
AZ Arizona	MD Maryland	OR Oregon
AR Arkansas	MA Massachusetts	PA Pennsylvania
CA California	MI Michigan	RI Rhode Island
CO Colorado	MN Minnesota	SC South Carolina
CT Connecticut	MS Mississippi	SD South Dakota
DE Delaware	MO Missouri	TN Tennessee
FL Florida	MT Montana	TX Texas
GA Georgia	NE Nebraska	UT Utah
HI Hawaii	NV Nevada	VT Vermont
ID Idaho	NH New Hampshire	VA Virginia
IL Illinois	NJ New Jersey	WA Washington
IN Indiana	NM New Mexico	WV West Virginia
IA Iowa	NY New York	WI Wisconsin
KS Kansas	NC North Carolina	WY Wyoming
KY Kentucky	ND North Dakota	

EXERCISE A: Using Abbreviations for the Names of States. In the blank, write the abbreviation for the state listed.

EXAMPLE: __VA__ Virginia

_____ 1. Hawaii   _____ 11. New Hampshire

_____ 2. North Dakota   _____ 12. Texas

_____ 3. Minnesota   _____ 13. Kansas

_____ 4. Oregon   _____ 14. Georgia

_____ 5. Utah   _____ 15. Arkansas

_____ 6. Iowa   _____ 16. Wyoming

_____ 7. Pennsylvania   _____ 17. Kentucky

_____ 8. Florida   _____ 18. Maryland

_____ 9. Rhode Island   _____ 19. Alaska

_____ 10. Delaware   _____ 20. Maine

EXERCISE B: More Practice Abbreviating the Names of States. Write the full name and the abbreviation for each state requested. Try not to use the same state twice.

EXAMPLE: Name a state on the East Coast.
    Massachusetts   _MA_

1. Name the state you live in. _____ _____

2. Name a state in the South. _____ _____

3. Name a state your relatives came from. _____ _____

4. Name a state spelled with four letters. _____ _____

5. Name a state you'd like to visit. _____ _____

6. Name a state close to the one you live in. _____ _____

7. Name a state in the West. _____ _____

8. Name a state with mountains. _____ _____

9. Name a great vacation state. _____ _____

10. Name a state that's small in area. _____ _____

28.4 Abbreviations for Time and Dates

In informal writing, you may use abbreviations for time and dates. Abbreviations for time begin with small letters and end with a period. On the other hand, abbreviations for days and months begin with a capital letter and end with a period.

ABBREVIATIONS FOR TIME AND DATES			
Time	**Days**	**Months**	
sec. second/s	Sun. Sunday	Jan. January	July July
min. minute/s	Mon. Monday	Feb. February	Aug. August
hr. hour/s	Tues. Tuesday	Mar. March	Sept. September
wk. week/s	Wed. Wednesday	Apr. April	Oct. October
mo. month/s	Thurs. Thursday	May May	Nov. November
yr. year/s	Fri. Friday	June June	Dec. December
a.m. before noon	Sat. Saturday		
p.m. after noon			

EXERCISE A: Abbreviating Time and Dates. In the blank, write the abbreviation for each item given.

EXAMPLE: ___*17 min. and 2 sec.*___ seventeen minutes and two seconds

_____ 1. Tuesday, May 17, 1952

_____ 2. eighteen months

_____ 3. eight o'clock in the morning

_____ 4. five years and three months

_____ 5. Thursday, August 19, 1844

_____ 6. three hours and 15 minutes

_____ 7. five o'clock in the afternoon

_____ 8. Saturday, November 22, 1923

_____ 9. two months three weeks and four days

_____ 10. Sunday, April 7, 1945

EXERCISE B: More Work with Abbreviating Time and Dates. Write out the full word for each abbreviation used in the sentences.

EXAMPLE: ___*Wednesday, March*___ The meeting is set for Wed., Mar. 2.

_____ 1. The baby is three wks. old today.

_____ 2. We spent two mo. and one wk. camping.

_____ 3. I was born Sat., Dec. 13, 1952.

_____ 4. Bobby just turned six yr. old.

_____ 5. Your payment is due Tues., Oct. 9.

_____ 6. I have a dentist appointment on Feb. 15.

_____ 7. That needs to cook for one hr. and ten min.

_____ 8. We were married on Sept. 27, 1981.

_____ 9. The race took me three hr. and nine min.

_____ 10. I'll call between 11 a.m. and 1 p.m.

28.5 Abbreviations for Measurements

Measurements—traditional and metric—are often abbreviated in informal writing and in mathematics and science. Abbreviate traditional measurements with a small letter at the beginning and a period at the end.

TRADITIONAL MEASUREMENTS					
in.	inch(es)	tsp.	teaspoon(s)	dr.	dram(s)
ft.	foot, feet	tbsp.	tablespoon(s)	oz.	ounce(s)
yd.	yard(s)	pt.	pint(s)	lb.	pound(s)
mi.	mile(s)	gal.	gallon(s)	F.	Fahrenheit

For metric measurements, begin with a small letter but do not end with a period.

METRIC MEASUREMENTS					
mm	millimeter(s)	mm	milligram(s)	L	liter(s)
cm	centimeter(s)	g	gram(s)	C	Celsius
m	meter(s)	kg	kilogram(s)		
km	kilometer(s)				

EXERCISE A: Abbreviating Measurements. In the blank, write the abbreviation for each item listed below. Use a numeral with each abbreviation.

EXAMPLE: ___2 tbsp.___ two tablespoons

_____ 1. one pint

_____ 2. two feet five inches

_____ 3. four pounds eight ounces

_____ 4. sixteen meters

_____ 5. twenty degrees Celsius

_____ 6. fifteen miles

_____ 7. eight gallons

_____ 8. sixty-three degrees Fahrenheit

_____ 9. three liters

_____ 10. three teaspoons

EXERCISE B: More Work Abbreviating Measurements. In the blank, write the abbreviation for each measurement listed below. Use a numeral with each abbreviation.

EXAMPLE: ___6 ft.___ a ladder six feet tall

_____ 1. a seven-pound three-ounce baby girl

_____ 2. four pounds of potatoes

_____ 3. a stifling forty degrees Celsius

_____ 4. three tablespoons of flour

_____ 5. a run of ten miles

_____ 6. a seven-foot one-inch basketball player

_____ 7. three centimeters of rain

_____ 8. a twenty-kilometer walk

_____ 9. two pints of whipping cream

_____ 10. four yards of material

29.1 Periods

A period should be used at the end of declarative and imperative sentences, indirect questions, and most abbreviations and initials.

USES OF A PERIOD	
With a declarative sentence	The rain washed out the road.
With an imperative sentence	Do your homework right now.
With an indirect question	The man asked me where the school was.
With an abbreviation	Prof. Joe Wall presented a slide show.
With initials	My accountant is R. L. Huntley.

EXERCISE A: Using Periods. Add periods wherever necessary.

EXAMPLE: Gov George Barthold won by a landslide
            Gov. George Barthold won by a landslide.

1. The restaurant is on Almond St just beyond the school
2. Dr D R Farnsworth will pull my wisdom teeth
3. Nancy J Spradling, please set the table now
4. Our newspaper asked when Sen Seth Robbins would arrive
5. I am short—only 5 ft 1 in tall in my stocking feet
6. My relatives have lived in Spokane, Wash for three years
7. Rep Teresa Willets asked about aid for Allendale Co residents
8. Buy me two lbs of bananas at the store
9. I asked what day of the week Mar 30 fell on
10. Bob asked if 10 C was equal to 50 F

EXERCISE B: More Practice Using Periods. Write the type of sentence indicated, using periods wherever necessary.

EXAMPLE: Imperative with an abbreviation
            Put in three tsp. of sugar.

1. Declarative with an abbreviation

_____

2. Imperative

_____

3. Indirect question

_____

4. Declarative with initials

_____

5. Imperative with an abbreviation

_____

29.2 Question Marks

The question mark is used in two places: at the end of an interrogative sentence and at the end of a word or phrase that asks a question. Do not make the mistake of using a question mark at the end of an indirect question.

USES OF THE QUESTION MARK	
Interrogative sentence	When does the newspaper arrive? Where are you staying?
Word or phrase that asks a question	You'll go to the store. When? He plans to climb that peak. How soon?

EXERCISE A: Using Question Marks. Place a question mark or period wherever necessary in the sentences below.

EXAMPLE: Do you want salad with dinner   Mashed potatoes
            Do you want salad with dinner?   Mashed potatoes?

1. When does that train come in   On what track

2. What were the problems faced by the Pilgrims in the New World

3. I asked when the report was due

4. I left a message for you to call me   Why didn't you

5. Are you going to Martha's to study   When

6. Can you figure out these directions

7. Dan asked if he could borrow the car   What did you say

8. What is your favorite dessert   Favorite movie

9. You said that Bret can help   If so, when

10. Which painting do you like the best

EXERCISE B: More Practice Using Question Marks. Place a question mark or period wherever necessary in the sentences below.

EXAMPLE: You made this cake   But for whom
            You made this cake. But for whom?

1. Why me   I'm already too busy

2. How long should I cook it   And at what temperature

3. I asked you what happened to the window   Did you break it

4. Come by around dinner   Is 6:00 p.m. convenient

5. Gerry said to meet after school   Where

6. Your arm is in a cast   For how long

7. The teacher asked what year WWII began   What would you answer

8. Did you lock the front door   Turn off the iron

9. We asked him about that   So what do you think he said

10. Can you organize these cards   By when

29.3 Exclamation Marks

An exclamation mark signals strong emotion or feeling. It should be used at the end of exclamatory sentences, strong or forceful imperative sentences, and interjections expressing strong emotion.

USES OF THE EXCLAMATION MARK	
Use an Exclamation Mark with:	**Example**
an exclamatory sentence	I got accepted to Stanford! We won first prize!
an imperative sentence that contains a forceful command	Stay out of the road! Do as I say!
an interjection expressing strong emotion	Ouch! That hurts. Wow! That rainbow is beautiful.

EXERCISE A: Using Exclamation Marks. Insert an exclamation mark where necessary. Then, tell what type of sentence it is, using the following code:

    1—exclamatory sentence   2—forceful imperative   3—strong interjection

EXAMPLE: _____ Catch that thief
             __2__ Catch that thief!

_____ 1. It's wonderful to see you looking so healthy

_____ 2. Hey   Come over here for a minute.

_____ 3. Gosh   I'm glad to see you.

_____ 4. Answer your father

_____ 5. Stop that man   He forgot his credit card.

_____ 6. Surprise   I bet you didn't know we were coming.

_____ 7. Your performance was breathtaking

_____ 8. Call the fire department

_____ 9. I'm completely exhausted

_____ 10. Run so you don't miss the bus

EXERCISE B: More Work with Exclamation Marks. If the use of the period and exclamation marks in the sentence is correct, write *C*. If it is incorrect, cross out the incorrect punctuation mark and put the proper one above it.

EXAMPLE: _____ Help me. I can't swim.

             _____ Help me ╳ I can't swim.
                          !

_____ 1. Read the first paragraph for us!

_____ 2. Oh my! You startled me at first.

_____ 3. What a wonderful vacation that was.

_____ 4. Wow. That was a photo-finish race.

_____ 5. I'm absolutely thrilled that you won the election!

_____ 6. Well. That guy is a poor sport.

_____ 7. Watch out for that car.

_____ 8. I washed my hair today!

_____ 9. Darn. I forgot my homework at home.

_____ 10. That's a splendid suggestion!

29.4 Commas in Compound Sentences

A compound sentence is formed from two simple sentences joined by a comma and a coordinating conjunction. The coordinating conjunctions are *and, but, for, nor, or, so,* and *yet.*

THE COMMA IN COMPOUND SENTENCES
Simple Sentence, Coordinating Conjunction, Simple Sentence
I ran after the ice-cream truck, *but* he didn't see me. Donald went to get hamburgers, *and* Margie set the table. Wendy turned the radio down, *so* I was finally able to study.

NOTE: If the two sentences forming the compound are very short, the comma can be omitted.

EXERCISE A: Using Commas in Compound Sentences. Insert the commas where necessary. Some sentences may not need a comma.

EXAMPLE: Nancy will handle the tickets and I will order the food.
           Nancy will handle the tickets, and I will order the food.

1. I called home for I was going to be very late.
2. Mom washed and Dad dried.
3. We can get dinner now or we can go to the movie.
4. Bill couldn't come today nor is he likely to come tomorrow.
5. The photographer grabbed his camera for the sunset was lovely.
6. I studied history for hours yet I still had trouble on the test.
7. She has never skiied before so I suggested that she take lessons.
8. The road was newly paved but the lines had yet to be painted on.
9. The car was just what I wanted and it was the right price.
10. The boy sang and the girl danced.

EXERCISE B: More Work Using Commas in Compound Sentences. Take the two sentences in each numbered item and join them into one compound sentence, using a comma and a conjunction.

EXAMPLE: *I pulled the weeds, and my brother mowed the lawn.*

1. We tried to make reservations tonight. The restaurant was booked.

_____

2. I enjoy preparing the salad. My mother likes to do the desserts.

_____

3. We must get this leak fixed. The whole basement might flood.

_____

4. I earned money babysitting. I was able to buy the concert tickets.

_____

5. We came out to practice soccer. The field was too wet.

_____

29.5 Commas in Series

A series is considered a list of three or more items. When a sentence contains a series of words or phrases, the items should be separated by commas.

COMMAS USED IN SERIES OF WORDS AND PHRASES	
Series of Words	I met the principal, the secretary, and the custodian. Apples, oranges, and bananas were all on sale.
Series of Phrases	The mouse ran across the floor, under the table, and out the door. The path takes us by the lake, through a pass, and into a meadow.

An exception to this rule is when each item in the series is followed by a conjunction; then no comma is used.

EXAMPLE: You can paint *or* color *or* draw.

EXERCISE A: Using Commas in Series. Insert commas into the sentences below wherever necessary. Some sentences may not require any commas.

EXAMPLE: You can paint scenery sew costumes or build sets.
You can paint scenery, sew costumes, or build sets.

1. The dog sniffed barked and growled at the stranger.
2. You can have eggs or cereal or French toast.
3. So far, we have driven through New Hampshire Vermont and Maine.
4. I grabbed my books rushed out the door and caught the bus.
5. The man sprayed the trees shrubs and the grass.
6. My dad plans to grow peanuts corn and hay this year.
7. Will you buy rent or lease a car?
8. The child had wandered out the door down the drive and into the street.
9. I addressed stamped and mailed the envelopes.
10. We can't decide whether to buy a boat or a raft or a kayak.

EXERCISE B: More Work Using Commas in a Series. Finish each sentence by adding a series that requires commas.

EXAMPLE: Every morning before school I . . .
Every morning before school, I _shower, dress, and eat._

1. At the beach I enjoy looking at . . .

_____

2. . . . are my favorite subjects in school.

_____

3. I plan to visit . . . this year.

_____

4. When I help around the house, I . . .

_____

5. . . . are the best shows on TV right now.

_____

29.6 Commas with Introductory Words and Phrases

A comma should be used after an introductory word or phrase. Introductory words include mild interjections *(oh, my, true)* or the name of a person you are addressing. Introductory phrases may be a prepositional phrase or a phrase that acts like another part of speech.

USING COMMAS WITH INTRODUCTORY WORDS AND PHRASES	
Introductory Words	My, that was a difficult workout. Bill, are you good at multiplication?
Introductory Phrases	In the morning, we'll go fishing. Blowing wildly in the wind, the trees weathered the fierce storm.

EXERCISE A: Recognizing Introductory Words and Phrases. Write the introductory word or phrase in each sentence and add the needed comma.

EXAMPLE: _No,_   No we don't have any sunglasses at this store.

_____ 1. With this freeze the crop will suffer.

_____ 2. To hear the speaker I moved up to the front.

_____ 3. Joan have you returned those library books?

_____ 4. During the night a storm developed.

_____ 5. Well your stroke looks a little sloppy.

_____ 6. Yes Marilyn can stay for dinner.

_____ 7. Calling my friends I got enough volunteers.

_____ 8. True we have a small budget for the project.

_____ 9. With your good attitude you'll get the job.

_____ 10. Jill turn off the radio.

EXERCISE B: Using Commas with Introductory Words and Phrases. Insert a comma wherever necessary into each sentence below.

EXAMPLE: No you can't have another snack before dinner.
          No, you can't have another snack before dinner.

1. Dressed in crazy costumes we went to a Halloween party.
2. With a loud crash the vase hit the marble floor.
3. Shawn do you think we have enough sand here?
4. Well your hem still seems to be a little uneven.
5. To get emergency help in our town you dial 411.
6. After a ten-minute delay the movie finally started.
7. Jason I'm over here next to the refreshment stand.
8. Yes I think you're right about that.
9. With this great invention I can make a fortune.
10. To memorize your speech you must go over it a number of times.

29.7 Commas with Interrupting Words and Phrases

Sometimes a word or phrase will interrupt the flow of the main sentence. Commas are placed around these words or phrases to set them off from the rest of the sentence. The commas show the reader that the information provided by the words and phrases, though helpful, is not essential to the main sentence.

USING COMMAS WITH INTERRUPTING WORDS AND PHRASES	
Interrupting Words and Phrases	**Example**
To name a person being addressed	She told you, *Joe*, to come at noon. When do the flags arrive, *Mr. Hall*?
To rename a noun	My sister, *the French major*, is graduating. The newt, *a small salamander*, ran into the water.
To set off a common expression	We will, *nevertheless*, continue to look. That book, *in my opinion*, will be a best-seller.

EXERCISE A: Recognizing Interrupting Words and Phrases. Write the interrupting word or phrase in each sentence, adding the commas.

EXAMPLE: *I believe,*   You are I believe here to see me.

_____ 1. Are you sure John that you added correctly?

_____ 2. My bike a ten-speed has a flat tire.

_____ 3. Mr. Penn our neighbor is selling his house.

_____ 4. That performance however is sold out.

_____ 5. I went to Disneyworld a theme park.

_____ 6. The design Mrs. Talbot looks good.

_____ 7. The road ahead I think is blocked.

_____ 8. The kilt a pleated skirt comes from Scotland.

_____ 9. Our friendship Melanie is important to me.

_____ 10. No operation is necessary in my opinion.

EXERCISE B: More Work with Interrupting Words and Phrases. Insert commas around the interrupting words or phrases in the sentences below.

EXAMPLE: You can be sure my friend that I will write.
          You can be sure, my friend, that I will write.

1. The elk a large deer is found in North America.
2. Are you sure Helen that you can't come swimming?
3. You need a haircut in my opinion.
4. Is it all right Dad if I use the power saw?
5. My grandmother a native of Ohio went back for a visit.
6. It is a crocodile not an alligator in that pond.
7. Your reservation it seems was canceled.
8. The dress is red my favorite color.
9. Boll weevils long-snouted beetles can damage cotton.
10. Advertising is necessary Mary if we want to sell our product.

29.8 Commas in Letters

Commas are used in three places in a friendly letter: the heading, the salutation, and the closing.

COMMAS IN LETTERS	
The heading	35 Andover Ct. Denver, Colorado 80204 (Between city and state) May 6, 1988 (After the number of the day)
The salutation	Dear Mr. Bloyd, (After the salutation)
The closing	With warm regards, (After the closing)

EXERCISE A: Using Commas in Letters. Insert a comma wherever necessary in the items below.

EXAMPLE: Dear Grandma Mavis
            Dear Grandma Mavis,

1. 894 Jenkins Blvd.
   Knoxville Tennessee 37901
   June 12 1986
2. Sincerely yours
3. Your friend
4. 56 Grant Ave.
   Mobile Alabama 36652
   October 19 1988
5. Dear Mr. Alberti

6. My dear Mrs. Martin
7. 469 Rowland Drive
   Wichita Kansas 67202
   January 13 1989
8. Yours truly
9. Dear Mom and Dad
10. 1444 Sutro Lane
    Pittsburg Pennsylvania 15219
    August 9 1986

EXERCISE B: More Work Using Commas in Letters. Write down the information requested, adding commas wherever necessary.

EXAMPLE: A salutation to a brother or sister
            Dear Leigh,

1. The heading for the address of a relative of yours

   _____

   _____

   _____

2. The salutation for a letter to your next-door neighbor

   _____

3. The closing for a letter to your grandparents

   _____

4. The heading for a letter from your school

   _____

   _____

   _____

5. The salutation for a letter to your teacher

   _____

29.9 Commas in Numbers

Knowing when to use commas with numbers can be confusing. Generally numbers of more than three *numerals* use commas to make them easier to read. Also numbers in series use commas to separate them.

NUMBERS WITH COMMAS	
More than three numerals	a crowd of 23,491; a cost of $497,322.00
Numbers in a series	Study pages 16, 19, and 23.

There are some large numbers that are exceptions to the rule and are not punctuated by commas.

NUMBERS WITHOUT COMMAS	
ZIP Code	36192
Telephone number	(800) 921-4343
Page number	Page 1142
Year	1999
Serial number	566 09 8638
House number	3035 Radcliff Avenue

EXERCISE A: Using Commas in Numbers. Rewrite the numbers in each sentence below, inserting commas where necessary. Some will not require commas.

EXAMPLE: ___16,500___ We can expect at least 16500 tickets to sell.

_____ 1. Our history book ends on page 1009.

_____ 2. Look at diagrams 7 8 and 9.

_____ 3. The carnival attracted 4500 people.

_____ 4. The library is located at 2788 Talbot Drive.

_____ 5. The length of the earth's equator is 24901.55 feet.

_____ 6. Call me at (415) 952-7341.

_____ 7. I will be twenty-one in 1996.

_____ 8. Check the glossary on pages 64 65 and 66.

_____ 9. A square mile is 27878400 square feet.

_____ 10. The longest river runs 4145 miles.

EXERCISE B: More Work Using Commas with Numbers. Fill in the requested information, inserting commas where necessary.

EXAMPLE: Your house number and address
  ___1694 Hanover Lane___

1. The amount of money you would like to earn in one year _____

2. Your ZIP code _____

3. An estimate of the number of miles on your family's car _____

4. Your telephone number _____

5. The number of pennies in $16.00 _____

30.1 Semicolons

An independent clause is like a complete sentence. It contains a subject and a verb. Two independent clauses closely related in meaning can be connected by a semicolon (;).

INDEPENDENT CLAUSES PUNCTUATED BY SEMICOLONS
Her tutoring certainly helped; I got an A on that test.
I did not mail the letter; I brought it over myself.
The courtroom was quiet; everyone waited with bated breath.

EXERCISE A: Using Semicolons. Make the two sentences of each numbered pair into one sentence joined by a semicolon.

EXAMPLE: ___*up; she*___ The deer looked up. She sensed my presence.

_____ 1. I vacuumed. My sister dusted.

_____ 2. The drums rolled. The trumpets blared.

_____ 3. The ground is wet. It must have rained last night.

_____ 4. The command was given. The dog snapped to attention.

_____ 5. Our train rocked gently. I was soon dozing.

_____ 6. The United States exports wheat. It imports oil.

_____ 7. It was a forbidding night. No moon was visible.

_____ 8. The team deserved to win. They played flawlessly.

_____ 9. I like Cajun food. I like it very much.

_____ 10. TV is boring. Give me a good book instead.

EXERCISE B: More Practice Using Semicolons. Add a semicolon and an independent clause to each independent clause already given below.

EXAMPLE: My sister is tall and blonde
_____*My sister is tall and blonde; I am short and brunette.*_____

1. I love sports _____

2. My mother wants me to baby-sit _____
_____

3. I have only six dollars _____

4. First we bought the paint _____

5. High school is different from elementary school _____
_____

30.2 Colons

 A colon is used primarily after an independent clause to introduce a list of items. The colon often follows such words as *the following, as follows, these,* or *those.* It is never used with a list that follows a verb or preposition. The colon also has some other uses.

USES OF THE COLON	
To introduce a list after an independent clause	You have your choice of three vegetables: corn, peas, or spinach.
To separate hours and minutes	8:40 a.m. 9:20 P.M.
After the salutation in a business letter	Dear Mr. Porter: Dear Mrs. Wilder:
On warnings and labels	Note: Keep refrigerated after opening.

EXERCISE A: Using Colons. Insert colons into the sentences below wherever they are needed. Some sentences may not need a colon.

EXAMPLE: I have packed the following a camera, an ice chest, and suitcases.
I have packed the following: a camera, an ice chest, and suitcases.

 1. The bottle read "Warning Keep out of the reach of children."
 2. Dear Miss Kashan
 3. *Masterpiece Theatre* can be seen at 11 00 a.m. and 9 00 p.m. on Friday.
 4. Some of people's fears include these spiders, the dark, and heights.
 5. For my birthday I got a stereo, a sweater, and a new book.
 6. My mother likes these magazines *Good Housekeeping*, *People*, and *Life*.
 7. Note These curtains may be ordered in other sizes.
 8. You must take the following classes English, history, and science.
 9. The following roads will be closed today Arden, Atherton, and Darnell.
10. Caution Roads Slippery When Wet

EXERCISE B: More Work Using Colons. Add the information requested below, using colons where needed.

EXAMPLE: I addressed the letter to . . .
I addressed the letter to "Gentlemen."

 1. Our family celebrates the following holidays . . .

_____

 2. Let's meet from . . . a.m. to . . . p.m.

_____

 3. The sign read " . . ."

_____

 4. My best features are these . . .

_____

 5. Some popular boys' (or girls') names include the following . . .

_____

30.3 Quotation Marks in Direct Quotation

Always use quotation marks to enclose a *direct quotation,* or a person's exact words. Using other punctuation—such as commas and end marks—will depend on whether the quotation also has a *he said* or *she said* phrase and where it is located in the quotation.

PUNCTUATING DIRECT QUOTATIONS	
Introductory words	The coach asked, "Will you be at practice?" The boy replied, "Sure, coach, I'll come."
Interrupting words	"I'm afraid," the officer said, "you were speeding." "Is there any chance," the driver asked, "that you could be mistaken?"
Concluding words	"Which dog is yours?" the woman inquired. "Mine is the Sheltie," the girl answered.

EXERCISE A: Using Quotation Marks in Direct Quotations. Insert quotation marks and commas where necessary in the sentences below.

EXAMPLE: Watch your step! Mother called.
            "Watch your step!" Mother called.

1. Benjamin Franklin wrote One today is worth two tomorrows.
2. Do I have to wear that stupid costume in the play? the boy complained.
3. What if my father worried I can't find the car keys?
4. We are going to visit an observatory the teacher announced.
5. Papyrus I wrote in my report was a kind of paper used by the Egyptians.
6. My sister shouted excitedly Here comes the parade!
7. Is it easier I asked for me to come to your house?
8. Do you want to play baseball during recess? Bob asked.
9. Our neighbor reported I watched a fascinating program on sharks.
10. Colton suggested Imitation is the sincerest form of flattery.

EXERCISE B: More Work Using Quotation Marks in Direct Quotations. Complete the sentences below, correctly punctuating the direct quotation and the *he said* or *she said* phrase.

EXAMPLE: My father asked . . .
            My father asked, *"What movie did you see?"*

1. . . . . my friend said.

_____

2. Our teacher explained . . . .

_____

3. . . . . I asked . . . .

_____

4. Our neighbor asked . . . .

_____

5. . . . . she shouted.

_____

30.4 Quotation Marks with Other Punctuation Marks

Commas and periods always go *inside* final quotation marks.

COMMAS AND PERIODS IN DIRECT QUOTATIONS	
Commas	"I found an oyster shell," Doris announced.
Periods	Jay said, "We should practice our skit."

The location of question marks and exclamation marks can vary. Place them inside the final quotation marks if they are part of the quotation. Place them outside if they are part of the complete sentence but not part of the quotation.

QUESTION MARKS AND EXCLAMATION MARKS IN DIRECT QUOTATIONS	
Inside the quotation marks	I asked, "When will we get there?" He cried, "That monkey bit me!"
Outside the quotation marks	Did you say, "Let's cut class tomorrow"? I have told you a hundred times, "Look before crossing the street"!

EXERCISE A: Using Quotation Marks with Other Punctuation. In the blank, write the punctuation mark and tell whether it should go inside or outside the quotation marks.

EXAMPLE: ___! inside___ Elsie pointed excitedly, "I see the ship"

_____ 1. The guide commented, "This is the throne"

_____ 2. "I made the team" Jim yelled happily.

_____ 3. "Lindbergh was a famous aviator" the teacher explained.

_____ 4. I asked, "How far is Mars from earth"

_____ 5. Please don't say "I ain't got it"

_____ 6. "We've got an emergency" the policeman shouted.

_____ 7. The child mumbled, "Let me stay at home"

_____ 8. Which one of you said, "I'm buying the food"

_____ 9. "Blackberries grow nearby" Jill said.

_____ 10. Why did you say, "That's a stupid idea"

EXERCISE B: Using Quotation Marks with Other Punctuation. Insert commas, periods, question marks, and exclamation marks wherever they are needed in the sentences below.

EXAMPLE: The cook asked, "Can someone hand me a sponge"
The cook asked, "Can someone hand me a sponge?"

1. "Run faster" my team cried.
2. I questioned, "Did you have your purse with you in the car"
3. We were ecstatic when the woman said, "Here is a little reward"
4. "I am nearsighted" George explained.
5. "Do you like my oil painting" the painter asked.
6. "I'll never trust you again" Nora shouted.
7. How did Kate know I said, "I'll surprise her with the present"
8. "We are growing almonds" Ruth told their visitors.
9. I cried sadly, "My project is a complete disaster"
10. The repairman reported, "The dishwasher is now fixed"

30.5 Quotation Marks for Dialogue

When punctuating dialogue, follow the general rules for using quotation marks, capital letters, and other punctuation marks. Start a new paragraph each time the speaker changes. If a speaker says two or more lines without interruption, put quotation marks at the beginning of the first sentence and at the end of the last one.

WRITING DIALOGUE

"I can hardly wait to see the Grand Canyon!" Mary said excitedly. "I hear it is beautiful."

"You won't be disappointed," her father commented. "I think you will find it as breathtaking as you imagine."

Her mother explained, "It looks just like the postcards you see. The colors are so vibrant. I think the Grand Canyon is nature's greatest oil painting!"

EXERCISE A: Using Quotation Marks for Dialogue. Put in quotation marks wherever they are needed in the following dialogue.

EXAMPLE: We had better get started now, the bus driver called.
   "We had better get started now," the bus driver called.

1. I hate taking swimming lessons every summer! Dorothy complained.
2. But why? Jessica inquired. I think swimming is lots of fun, especially in warm weather.
3. Oh, they always force you to do things you don't want to. Last year they made me do a back dive and I did a belly flop!
4. I'll bet it wasn't that bad, Jessica said. You're probably just exaggerating it.
5. You think so? Well, how would you feel if you had two hundred people watching you from a viewing stand? Believe me, it was embarrassing!

EXERCISE B: Paragraphing Dialogue. Circle the first word in each sentence that requires indentation for a new paragraph.

   "What can we get Dad for his birthday?" Bob asked. "Unfortunately," Nicole said, "I haven't got a clue. He is the most difficult person to buy for!" "Last year we got him slippers. The year before that it was a magazine subscription," recalled Bob. Nicole sighed, "Not very exciting, huh? Wait, I've got it. He loves to fish. How about giving him a certificate for a day on one of those fishing boats?" "Now that's more like it. I think he would love it," Bob exclaimed. "Let's do it!"

30.6 Underlining and Quotation Marks in Titles

Some titles and names are underlined while others are enclosed in quotation marks. The charts below give examples of each.

TITLES THAT ARE UNDERLINED	
Books	<u>Fahrenheit 451</u>
Plays	<u>You Can't Take It with You</u>
Magazines and Newspapers	<u>Smithsonian</u>, <u>Wall Street Journal</u>
Movies	<u>E.T.</u>
Television Series	<u>Sesame Street</u>
Paintings and Sculptures	<u>Mona Lisa</u>, <u>The Thinker</u>
Air and Space Vehicles	<u>Spitfire</u>, <u>Apollo 8</u>
Ships and Trains	<u>Oriana</u>, <u>Embassy</u>

TITLES THAT ARE ENCLOSED IN QUOTATION MARKS	
Stories	"The Lottery"
Chapters	"Getting Ideas for Speeches"
Articles	"A Mother's Fight for Justice"
Episodes	"Hawaii: The Crucible of Life" (an episode from the <u>Nova</u> series)
Songs	"Take Me Out to the Ball Game"

EXERCISE A: Using Underlining and Quotation Marks. Underline or enclose in quotation marks each of the titles or names given below.

EXAMPLE: A Trap (short story)
           "A Trap"

1. Nite Owl (train)
2. The Secret Garden (book)
3. The Artist's Studio (painting)
4. Blue Moon (song)
5. The Witness (movie)

6. Bull's Eye! (article)
7. I Love Lucy (TV series)
8. Viking I (spacecraft)
9. The Monkey's Paw (short story)
10. Our Town (play)

EXERCISE B: More Practice Using Underlining and Quotation Marks. Write in the blank whether the title or name in the sentence needs *underlining* or *quotation marks*.

EXAMPLE: ___underlining___ I like to read Sports Illustrated.

_____ 1. The artist Donatello did the statue St. George.

_____ 2. I watched Forest in the Clouds from the *Nature* series.

_____ 3. The Russian spacecraft Salyut 7 was in space for over 211 days.

_____ 4. We are to read the chapter called Learning the Keyboard.

_____ 5. They wrote a song about the train, called The Santa Fe.

_____ 6. Have you read the novel Exodus, by Leon Uris?

_____ 7. We read the Raleigh Times.

_____ 8. I still enjoy watching re-runs of M.A.S.H.

_____ 9. Manet painted Luncheon on the Grass.

_____ 10. My Dad always sings Yesterday.

30.7 Hyphens in Numbers and Words

Numbers and words often contain hyphens.

HYPHENS IN NUMBERS		
Use a Hyphen When You Write	**Example**	
the numbers twenty-one through ninety-nine	forty-six	eighty-seven
a fraction used as an adjective	The race was one-third over.	

HYPHENS IN WORDS		
Use a Hyphen	**Example**	
after a prefix followed by a proper noun or adjective	mid-July	pro-American
with the prefixes *all-, ex-, self-,* and the suffix *-elect*	ex-Senator self-appointed	all-league President-elect
with compound modifiers	around-the-clock	fifty-fifty

EXERCISE A: Using Hyphens in Numbers and Words. Rewrite the word or number in each phrase that requires a hyphen, inserting the hyphen. If the phrase requires no hyphen, write *C* in the blank.

EXAMPLE: _____*anti-nuclear*_____ the anti nuclear movement

_____ 1. one half of the money

_____ 2. the all star game

_____ 3. feeling put upon by friends

_____ 4. an excited ex felon

_____ 5. thirty seven late entries

_____ 6. one third water and two thirds vinegar

_____ 7. a pro Mexican soccer crowd

_____ 8. ate raw sea urchins

_____ 9. a second rate job

_____ 10. a self winding watch

EXERCISE B: More Practice Using Hyphens. Insert hyphens where necessary. If no hyphen is necessary, write *C* in the blank.

_____ 1. He was voted all around best athlete.

_____ 2. I was elected sergeant at arms.

_____ 3. The stadium was two thirds full.

_____ 4. We have to move by mid March.

_____ 5. That was in the post Kennedy era.

_____ 6. You must meet with the treasurer elect.

_____ 7. It was the best selling novel of the year.

_____ 8. I need twenty five volunteers for the charity auction.

_____ 9. My grandfather was a self educated man.

_____ 10. We sat in the dining room for dessert.

30.8 Hyphens at the Ends of Lines

If a word must be divided at the end of a line, the general rule is to divide it only between syllables. The dictionary should be used when you are unsure where the syllables fall. Several other rules will also help you hyphenate words correctly at the ends of lines.

FOUR RULES FOR WORD DIVISION

1. Never divide a one-syllable word.
   Incorrect: It was a frei-   Correct: It was a freight
            ght train.   train.
2. Never divide a word so that one letter stands alone.
   Incorrect: I was all a   Correct: I was all alone.
            lone.
3. Never divide proper nouns or proper adjectives.
   Incorrect: Rem-   Correct: Rembrandt
            brandt painted this.   painted this.
4. Divide a hyphenated word only after the hyphen.
   Incorrect: I bought thir-   Correct: I bought thirty-
            ty-five balloons.   five balloons.

EXERCISE A: Using Hyphens to Divide Words. Rewrite each word, inserting a hyphen to show where the word can be divided. If the word cannot be divided, leave it untouched.

EXAMPLE: ___*gas-light*___ gaslight
_____ 1. juicy
_____ 2. magic
_____ 3. self-control
_____ 4. Spanish
_____ 5. nugget
_____ 6. elect
_____ 7. penance
_____ 8. Yellowstone
_____ 9. project
_____ 10. mid-September

EXERCISE B: More Practice Hyphenating at the Ends of Lines. Draw vertical lines between syllables that can be divided at the end of a line. Circle words that should not be divided at the end of a line.

EXAMPLE: forest for|est   walked (walked)

1. evict
2. custom
3. Bolivia
4. legal
5. noise
6. tasty
7. Grandmother
8. stillness
9. kept
10. boiler

11. doorway
12. column
13. blazed
14. all-time
15. passage
16. scenic
17. pro-German
18. maintain
19. neutral
20. about

105

30.9 Apostrophes Used to Show Ownership

To show ownership or possession, an apostrophe and sometimes an -s are used.

FORMING POSSESSIVES	
Forming the Possessive	**Example**
Add 's to singular nouns	Mother's book teacher's comment
Add 's to singular nouns ending in s	chorus's trophy Kris's paper (Exception: If there are too many s sounds, drop the last s. Example: Dickens' novel)
Add an apostrophe to plurals ending in s	cats' howling friends' reunion
Add 's to plurals not ending in s	geese's food children's toys

EXERCISE A: Using Apostrophes to Show Ownership. Write the possessive form of each phrase in the space provided.

EXAMPLE: the presentation of the group _____the group's presentation_____

1. the curls of the lass _____

2. the nest of the birds _____

3. the blanket of the child _____

4. the response of the crowd _____

5. the calendar of the doctor _____

6. the ruling of the officials _____

7. the feed of the chickens _____

8. the help of the clerk _____

9. the bracelet of Tess _____

10. the vote of the women _____

EXERCISE B: More Practice Using Apostrophes to Show Ownership. Write the possessive form of each underlined noun in the blank provided.

EXAMPLE: _____deputy's_____ I followed the deputy suggestion.

_____ 1. We have to gather the sheep wool.

_____ 2. I read the writer latest biography.

_____ 3. Next week is the Governors conference.

_____ 4. The Jenkins party is next week.

_____ 5. We are going camping in our friends trailer.

_____ 6. I want to see the class new computer.

_____ 7. You should follow the lawyer advice.

_____ 8. It's time to harvest the farmers crops.

_____ 9. Bill is going to the annual men barbecue.

_____ 10. Our neighbors house needs painting.

30.10 Apostrophes in Contractions

In a contraction, the apostrophe shows where one or more letters have been omitted. Generally, contractions are used in informal writing.

COMMONLY USED CONTRACTIONS		
aren't (are not) isn't (is not) wasn't (was not) weren't (were not) hasn't (has not)	haven't (have not) hadn't (had not) can't (cannot) couldn't (could not) didn't (did not)	don't (do not) doesn't (does not) shouldn't (should not) won't (will not) wouldn't (would not)
I'll (I will) you'll (you will)	he'll (he will) she'll (she will)	we'll (we will) they'll (they will)
I'm (I am) you're (you are) he's (he is) she's (she is)	it's (it is) we're (we are) they're (they are) who's (who is)	where's (where is) John's (John is)
I'd (I would) you'd (you would) he'd (he would)	she'd (she would) we'd (we would) they'd (they would)	who'd (who would) Sara'd (Sara would)

EXERCISE A: Using Apostrophes in Contractions. In the blank, write the contractions that would be used in place of the underlined words.

EXAMPLE: _____doesn't_____ She <u>does not</u> practice the piano enough.

_____ 1. <u>Who is</u> that in the red coat?

_____ 2. <u>They would</u> have told me.

_____ 3. Martha will do it if <u>he will</u> do it too.

_____ 4. That gas station <u>would not</u> take checks.

_____ 5. <u>Nancy is</u> already in the car.

_____ 6. The paint <u>was not</u> dry.

_____ 7. I think <u>he would</u> be able to fix the car.

_____ 8. If <u>you are</u> in town, stop by.

_____ 9. The meat <u>should not</u> be frozen.

_____ 10. I <u>have not</u> heard that song.

EXERCISE B: More Practice with Apostrophes in Contractions. In the blank, write the words that can be used in place of the underlined contraction.

EXAMPLE: _____she is_____ The teacher said that <u>she's</u> next.

_____ 1. <u>I'd</u> go if I could.

_____ 2. He <u>won't</u> tell your great news.

_____ 3. If <u>you're</u> not ready, you will not pass.

_____ 4. I <u>couldn't</u> find the shoes I wanted.

_____ 5. The baby sitter <u>can't</u> stay.

_____ 6. <u>He'll</u> bring the slide projector.

_____ 7. <u>George'd</u> get the groceries.

_____ 8. My Dad called, "<u>They're</u> here!"

_____ 9. Tonight <u>I'll</u> letter the signs.

_____ 10. I <u>wouldn't</u> try that if I were you.

30.11 Avoiding Problems with Apostrophes

Sometimes the apostrophe is used incorrectly. Remember, never use an apostrophe with possessive personal pronouns.

POSSESSIVE PERSONAL PRONOUNS		
my	his	our
mine	her	ours
your	hers	their
yours	its	theirs

Do not confuse *its* and *it's*, *theirs* and *there's*, *whose* and *who's*, or *your* and *you're*. Remember that those containing the apostrophes stand for the contractions *it is*, *there is*, *who is*, and *you are*.

EXERCISE A: Using Apostrophes Where Necessary. Circle the correct choice of the two given in parentheses.

EXAMPLE: I ate the rest of (yours, your's).

1. (Its, It's) your turn at bat.
2. The child wanted (hers, her's) immediately.
3. (Whose, who's) notebook is this?
4. Look, (theirs, there's) the lake!
5. Maybe we will get (ours, our's) tomorrow.
6. (Your, You're) friend is at the door.
7. I thought (his, his') science project was excellent.
8. Will (yours, your's) look like that drawing?
9. (Theirs, There's) is the red van with the flat tire.
10. I feel (your, you're) going to win the scholarship.

EXERCISE B: More Practice Avoiding Apostrophe Errors. Write a sentence correctly using the word listed.

EXAMPLE: it's
      I heard that it's supposed to rain.

1. there's

_____

2. whose

_____

3. you're

_____

4. its

_____

5. who's

_____

31.1 Prewriting

Prewriting is the planning that you do before you start to write. The following chart presents the basic steps of prewriting.

THE STEPS OF PREWRITING

1. Explore ideas for writing topics using such techniques as brainstorming, free writing, and journal writing.
2. Choose a topic from the ideas you have gathered. It should be narrow and specific enough for you to cover it in the space available.
3. Identify your audience. Will you be writing for your teacher, classmates, readers of the school newspaper, adults, others?
4. Decide whether your purpose will be to inform, to persuade, or to entertain.
5. State in a sentence the most important idea you wish to express.
6. Gather together the examples, details, or incidents you will use to support your main idea.
7. Organize your supporting information in chronological order, spatial order, or order of importance.

EXERCISE A: Planning a Review. Imagine that you have been asked to write a review of a record album, movie, or TV show for your school newspaper. The review is to be no more than 150 words. It will be read mostly by the students of your school. First, choose the record, movie, or TV show you will review. Then use the blank space below to brainstorm for ideas. Jot down all the things you might want to say, including possible main ideas.

_____

_____

_____

_____

_____

_____

_____

_____

_____

EXERCISE B: Further Planning. On the line labeled *Main Idea*, write down the most important thing you have to say about what you are reviewing. Then use the lines below to write down the ideas, examples, and details you will use to support your main idea. Finally, number these supporting items in the order in which you will use them.

Main Idea _____

_____

_____

_____

_____

_____

_____

_____

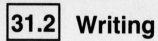

Writing

When you have written down a statement of your main idea and arranged your supporting information, you can write your first draft.

WRITING A FIRST DRAFT
1. Normally, begin by stating your main idea.
2. Then support your main idea with the examples, details, or incidents you have chosen, following the order you have decided to use.
3. Change your arrangement of supporting information if a different arrangement seems better.
4. Change, or add to, the examples, details, or incidents you have chosen if better ones come to mind.
5. Remove those examples, details, or incidents that seem less useful than any of the new ones you have thought of.
6. Keep in mind your audience and purpose—whom you are writing for and why you are writing.

EXERCISE A: Writing a Review. Using the work you did for Exercises A and B on the preceding page, write a first draft of your review.

_____

_____

_____

_____

_____

_____

_____

_____

_____

_____

_____

EXERCISE B: More Work with Your First Draft. Put your draft aside for a while. Then do the following with it.

1. Read the review aloud to yourself, listening for problems. What weaknesses did you find?

_____

_____

2. Read the review to a classmate. What is your listener's opinion of it?

_____

_____

3. Ask another person to read the review. What weaknesses did you notice while you were listening?

_____

_____

4. Ask someone else to read your review silently and then to offer an opinion of it. What was this reader's opinion? _____

_____

_____

31.3 Revising

Revising involves (1) revising for sense and (2) revising for word choice and sentence variety. Always proofread your work before submitting it.

REVISING FOR SENSE

1. Check that the main idea is stated clearly.
2. Check that the supporting ideas, examples, and details are effective.
3. Remove those that are unrelated to the main idea.
4. Decide whether the supporting items are arranged in the best way.

REVISING FOR WORD CHOICE AND SENTENCE VARIETY

1. Check that you have used the clearest, most exact words for your ideas.
2. Check that the language is appropriate for your readers.
3. Check that the meaning of each sentence is clear.
4. Go over your sentences for variety of length and structure.

EXERCISE A: Revising Your Review. Using the first chart above, revise your review for sense. Then, using the second chart, revise it for word choice and sentence variety. Make use of the opinions you gathered for Exercise B on the preceding page.

EXERCISE B: Writing the Final Version. Write a clean, neat final copy of your review. Proofread it carefully for errors in usage and mechanics.

_____

_____

_____

_____

_____

_____

_____

_____

_____

_____

_____

_____

_____

_____

_____

_____

_____

_____

_____

_____

32.1 Using Action Words

Use action verbs to express ideas clearly and forcefully.

REPLACING LINKING VERBS WITH ACTION VERBS	
Sentences with Linking Verbs	**Sentences with Action Verbs**
The Lions Club *was* the sponsor of the festival.	The Lions Club *sponsored* the festival.
Lauren's parents *were* pleased with her report card.	Lauren's report card *pleased* her report card.
Their greeting *was* warm.	They *greeted* us warmly.

EXERCISE A: Using Action Verbs. Rewrite each of the following sentences using the action verb in parentheses.

EXAMPLE: Angie's questions were an annoyance to her parents.   (annoyed)
     Angie's questions annoyed her parents.

1. Mr. DeAngelo is a builder of houses.   (builds)

_____

2. The monument is an attraction for thousands of tourists.   (attracts)

_____

3. Kevin was a volunteer for the clean-up committee.   (volunteered)

_____

4. The new plant will be an employer for thousands.   (will employ)

_____

5. The sauce has a spicy taste.   (tastes)

_____

EXERCISE B: More Work with Action Verbs. Rewrite each sentence as needed to use an action verb as the main verb.

EXAMPLE: The class was confused by the directions.
     The directions confused the class.

1. Sandy will be the representative from our school at the convention.

_____

2. The baby usually is asleep most of the afternoon.

_____

3. My father is a teacher of art at the state college.

_____

4. That chef is a specialist in Mexican food.

_____

5. The water supply in that reservoir may soon be exhausted by careless users.

_____

32.2 Using Specific Words

Choose specific nouns, verbs, adjectives, and adverbs.

Vague Words	Specific Words
The *pet* watched the *fish*. (nouns)	The *Siamese cat* watched the *goldfish*.
The goldfish *went* back and forth. (verb)	The goldfish *darted* back and forth.
The cat eyed the fish in the *nice* pool. (adjective)	The cat eyed the fish in the *clear, sparkling* pool.
Then the cat flipped its paw *in*. (adverbs)	*Suddenly* the cat flipped its paw *downward*.

EXERCISE A: Using Specific Words. On the blank after each sentence, write a specific word or word group to replace the underlined word(s).

EXAMPLE: I <u>got</u> the vegetables <u>ready</u> for dinner. _*rinsed and scrubbed*_

1. We ordered <u>meat</u> and a salad. _____

2. The <u>thing</u> rose into the clouds high above us. _____

3. The <u>wind</u> rustled the leaves on the trees. _____

4. The <u>weather</u> broke previous records for high temperatures throughout the Southwest.
   _____

5. A <u>small animal</u> darted under the wood pile. _____

6. What is a birthday party without <u>dessert</u>? _____

7. Marnie <u>did</u> the puzzle quickly. _____

8. The <u>sound</u> startled the by-standers. _____

9. Bonnie has a <u>nice</u> smile. _____

10. Thousands attended the <u>event</u> in the park. _____

EXERCISE B: More Work with Specific Words. Underline any vague words in each sentence below. Then rewrite the sentence, replacing the vague words with more specific ones.

EXAMPLE: The <u>group</u> is <u>doing something</u> to make money for <u>a good cause</u>.
The Rotary Club is sponsoring a pancake breakfast to raise money for the flood victims.

1. The pirate's bird said something.

   _____

2. Some plants grow well in the desert.

   _____

3. After our long hike in the August heat, a drink was refreshing.

   _____

4. A bird was on a branch of a tree.

   _____

5. The dog messed with its toy.

   _____

32.3 Avoiding Slang

Avoid slang in your writing.

Slang	Revised
Steve is really *into* motorcycles. Audrey was *uptight* about her math test. The consumer reporter tries to help people avoid being *ripped off*.	Steve is very *interested in* motorcycles. Audrey was *worried* about her math test. The consumer reporter tries to help people avoid being *cheated*.

EXERCISE A: Finding and Replacing Slang. Underline the slang word or expression in each sentence. On the line after the sentence, write a standard English word or phrase to replace the slang.

EXAMPLE: Ed <u>beat it out of here</u> as soon as my parents came home. ___*left*___

1. Karen's old man is really strict. _____

2. To win Lou's favor, Huey took the rap for him. _____

3. Phil often looks spacy during history class. _____

4. The campers were really wiped out by all the exercise. _____

5. That story Donna told really cracked me up. _____

6. The representative conned us into buying more than we needed. _____

7. My parents think my friend Waldo is a weirdo. _____

8. Elsa wears some pretty far-out clothes sometimes. _____

9. The advertisers hyped the concert as the event of the decade. _____

10. The first piece that the pianist played really bowled me over. _____

EXERCISE B: More Work with Slang. Rewrite each sentence below, replacing any slang words or expressions with standard English.

EXAMPLE: Jan was really bummed out over his report card.
   Jan was really upset about his report card.

1. Betsy has a hang-up about crossing bridges.

_____

2. Len really gets bent out of shape when someone criticizes him.

_____

3. That car has been a lemon since the day we got it.

_____

4. We better hit the road, or we will be late.

_____

5. Carl and Danny really pigged out on pancakes yesterday.

_____

33.1 Sentence Combining

Combine two or three short, choppy sentences into one longer sentence.

WAYS OF COMBINING SENTENCES	
Short Sentences	**Combined Sentence**
Arthur is taking tennis lessons. Louise is taking tennis lessons.	Arthur and Louise are taking tennis lessons. (compound subject)
Paul sat in his room. Paul read a book.	Paul sat in his room and read a book. (compound predicate)
We waited. The bus never came.	We waited, but the bus never came. (compound sentence)
Our new car is very economical. It is a small, compact model.	Our new car, a small compact model, is very economical. (appositive phrase)
We saw Jason last night. He was at the movie.	We saw Jason last night at the movie. (prepositional phrase)
Fluffy was dozing by the fire. She looked quite content.	Dozing by the fire, Fluffy looked quite content. (participial phrase)

EXERCISE A: Combining Sentences. Using the methods above, rewrite each group of sentences below as a single sentence.

EXAMPLE: Maine moose have huge noses. They have big droopy mouths. They are funny-looking animals.

   Maine moose, funny-looking animals, have huge noses and big droopy mouths.

1. The weather may clear. We may go sailing after all.

   _____

2. Last night Marcia called. She invited me to spend the day.

   _____

3. My father is building us a playhouse. My grandfather is helping him.

   _____

4. Jennie went to the movies. Sue went, too. I went with them.

   _____

5. The cookies smelled delicious. They were baking in the oven.

   _____

EXERCISE B: More Work with Combining Sentences. Follow the directions for Exercise A.

1. We were able to assemble the bicycle ourselves. We followed the directions carefully.

   _____

2. The horse got out of the barn. It ran across the field. It went into the woods.

   _____

3. The concert tickets raised lots of money. The album made money, too.

   _____

4. Mr. Gordon demands the best from the players. He is the girl's basketball coach.

   _____

5. Jogging is good exercise. Swimming is good exercise. Biking is good, too.

   _____

33.2 Adding Details to Sentences

Enrich short sentences by adding details to the subject, verb, or complement.

LENGTHENING SHORT SENTENCES BY ADDING DETAILS	
Adding Details to the Subject	
The kitten was terrified.	Trapped in the tree with the Doberman barking below, the kitten was terrified.
Adding Details to the Verb	
The gardener trimmed the shrubs.	The gardener carefully and lovingly trimmed the shrubs.
Adding Details to the Complement	
The explorers found a treasure chest.	The explorers found an old, moldy treasure chest with a pile of rocks inside it.

EXERCISE A: Adding Details to Short Sentences. Rewrite each sentence by adding the details in parentheses where they fit best.

EXAMPLE: The ship flew a flag. (pirate, with a skull and crossbones)
The pirate ship flew a flag with a skull and crossbones.

1. The students are making plans. (high school, elaborate, for the prom)

_____

2. Fish swam in the tank. (Colorful, tropical; large salt-water)

_____

3. The restaurant was full. (new Mexican, of happy, chattering customers)

_____

4. Judy decided to enter the race. (In spite of her trainer's advice, annual long-distance)

_____

5. The house is on a beautiful lot. (old colonial, wooded, with many pine trees)

_____

EXERCISE B: More Work with Short Sentences. Rewrite each sentence below by adding at least two details of your own.

EXAMPLE: The politician attracted many supporters.
The dynamic young politician attracted many supporters among people from various
backgrounds.

1. The movie scared the child.

_____

2. We enjoyed the meal.

_____

3. Flowers cover the fence.

_____

4. Tim hated camp.

_____

5. Kelly's story had good details.

_____

33.3 Shortening Rambling Sentences

Separate a rambling compound sentence into two or more shorter sentences.

Rambling Sentences	Revised Sentences
We had planned a family reunion, and everyone was going to bring something, but my cousins got sick, so my aunt and uncle couldn't come, and we postponed the whole thing for a month.	We had planned a family reunion, and everyone was going to bring something. However, my cousins got sick, so my aunt and uncle couldn't come. We postponed the reunion for a month.
The batter stepped up to the plate and took a few practice swings, and the pitcher took the set position, but the batter stepped out of the box, and after a few more repeats of this, the fans began to boo.	The batter stepped up to the plate and took a few practice swings. Then the pitcher took the set position, but the batter stepped out of the box. After a few more repeats of this, the fans began to boo.

EXERCISE A: Shortening Rambling Sentences. Rewrite the rambling sentence below to make two or more shorter ones.

EXAMPLE: I heard the doorbell ring, so I put down my book and went to answer it, but when I got there, I didn't see anyone, so I went back to my book, and once again the bell rang, but this time when I got there I found a beautiful basket of flowers.

I heard the doorbell ring, so I put down my book and went to answer it. When I got there and didn't see anyone, I went back to my book. Once again the bell rang. This time when I got there I found a beautiful basket of flowers.

Audrey is always very careful about getting assignments down clearly, so she was the best person to call with my question, but she wasn't home, so I tried Angie, but she wasn't home either, and by the time I could reach anyone the library was closed, so I couldn't do the work anyway.

_____

_____

_____

_____

EXERCISE B: More Work with Shortening Rambling Sentences. Follow the directions for Exercise A.

We walked for miles through the woods, and we finally found a campsite that we liked, so we pitched our tent beside the stream, and Dad went off to fill the water buckets while we gathered sticks for kindling, and when we came back to camp, the tent was on the ground, and a raccoon was eating our bread and graham crackers.

_____

_____

_____

_____

_____

34.1 Topic Sentences

The topic sentence expresses the main idea of a paragraph.

Topic Sentence	Support
Popcorn is different from other kinds of corn.	Its kernels have a hard waterproof covering that keeps moisture in. When the kernels are heated, the moisture turns to steam, which makes the kernels explode. The result is puffy popcorn.

EXERCISE A: Recognizing Topic Sentences. Circle the letter of the topic sentence in each group below.

EXAMPLE: a. African elephants are larger than Indian elephants.
b. African elephants have larger ears than Indian elephants.
c. Female African elephants have tusks, but female Indian elephants usually do not.
d. There are several differences between African elephants and Indian elephants.

1. a. Mercury, Venus, Earth, and Mars are known as the terrestrial, or land, planets.
   b. Jupiter, Saturn, Neptune, and Uranus are the gas giants.
   c. Nine planets make up our solar system.
   d. Faraway Pluto is the least well-known planet.

2. a. Handcrafts courses such as pottery, macramé, and basketry are very popular.
   b. Summer school offers more than boring make-up courses.
   c. Sports clinics attract many students as well.
   d. Far and away the courses that are most in demand are those in computers.

3. a. Musk glands in the skunk's body store a powerful fluid.
   b. When danger approaches, the skunk shoots out this fluid—sometimes as far as fifteen or twenty feet.
   c. The smell of the skunk's spray is extremely difficult to get out of clothing, but the chemicals in it are truly harmful to the skin and eyes of humans.
   d. Skunks have a unique way of defending themselves.

EXERCISE B: More Work with Recognizing Topic Sentences. Follow the directions for Exercise A.

1. a. Wendell Morningstar, of Delaware County, Ohio, collects wooden nickels.
   b. Mrs. Beatrice Warburton, of Westboro, Massachusetts, has bred more than 90 new varieties of irises.
   c. Many people have unusual hobbies.
   d. Victorian cooking is the hobby of Linda Moss, of Richmond, Virginia.

2. a. Huskies' thick coats and a layer of fat protect them from the cold.
   b. These dogs are able to find their way through driving snow and blinding blizzards.
   c. Male huskies usually do most of the heavy work, such as pulling loads, while females remain at home for protection.
   d. Huskies are useful dogs for people in arctic climates.

34.2 Supporting Topic Sentences with Examples

Use examples to clarify or illustrate a topic sentence.

Topic Sentence	Examples
There are many interesting things to do at Walt Disney World.	There are a number of different boat rides and a ride called the Teacup. The haunted house and racing cars are also fun. You mingle with the Disney characters walking through the park, and you watch them perform in shows.

EXERCISE A: Finding Examples to Support Topic Sentences. Assume that each sentence below is a topic sentence for a paragraph. For each one, write three examples that clarify, illustrate, or support the topic sentence.

EXAMPLE: A variety of healthful foods is important to good health.
   Dairy products, rich in calcium, help build strong teeth and bones.
   Fruits and vegetables are rich in vitamins and minerals.
   Carbohydrates are good sources of quick energy.

1. Team sports can build more than physical skills.

   _____

   _____

   _____

2. Campers must be prepared for a wide range of experiences.

   _____

   _____

   _____

3. Some TV commercials are more entertaining than the shows they sponsor.

   _____

   _____

   _____

EXERCISE B: More Work with Supporting Examples. Follow the directions for Exercise A.

1. Care and planning can prevent most accidents in the home.

   _____

   _____

   _____

2. Many different kinds of water sports are popular today.

   _____

   _____

   _____

34.3 Supporting Topic Sentences with Details

Use details to develop a topic sentence vividly.

Topic Sentence	Details
It was a perfect day for our class trip to the shore.	The sky was bright blue with only a few puffy white clouds. The sun shone brilliantly, and the day was hot. A breeze from off the water, however, would keep us cool.

EXERCISE A: Finding Details to Support a Topic Sentence. Assume that each sentence below is a topic sentence for a paragraph. For each one, write three details that illustrate or support the topic sentence.

EXAMPLE: All of Doug's symptoms suggested that he had flu.
        He had felt tired and achy all day.
        He had chills, a runny nose, a scratchy throat, and a slight cough.
        When he checked his temperature, it was 102°F.

1. Helen's necklace is very unusual.

_____

_____

_____

2. The pop-up camper held everything we would need for our traveling home.

_____

_____

_____

3. The best thing at the amusement park was the haunted house.

_____

_____

_____

EXERCISE B: More Work with Supporting Details. Follow the directions for Exercise A.

1. The view from the top of the mountain was breathtaking.

_____

_____

2. The most appealing thing there was the beautiful garden.

_____

_____

_____

34.4 Supporting Topic Sentences with Incidents

Use an incident, or brief story, to support a paragraph's main idea.

Topic Sentence	Incident
Many people suffer from narcolepsy, an uncontrollable need to sleep.	Uncle Jack had one spell that was the worst I have ever heard of. Once, while dining with friends in a Chinese restaurant, he fell asleep at the table. His hand settled in the plate of the woman next to him. She had to maneuver her chopsticks between his fingers.

EXERCISE A: Using an Incident to Develop a Topic Sentence. Assume that each sentence below is a topic sentence for a paragraph. Choose one, write it in the space below, and write an incident to support it.

EXAMPLE: Mr. Jackson always takes time to meet his students' special needs.
Mr. Jackson always takes time to meet his students' special needs. In November, I had pneumonia and missed a month of school. Mr. Jackson met once a week with the home tutor to be sure I was keeping up with the class assignments. When I returned to school he spent his planning periods and breaks working with me for the first week. That way I could catch up on some of the special things the class had done while I was out.

1. Some of the best gifts don't have to cost anything at all.
2. Misunderstandings often occur when someone is learning a new language.
3. Remaining calm in a crisis can save a life.
4. Celebrities often give their time and talents to worthy causes.
5. Aunt Helen can prepare a company dinner from leftovers on a moment's notice.

_____

_____

_____

_____

_____

EXERCISE B: More Work with Using Incidents for Support. Follow the directions for Exercise A.

1. Dogs are known as "man's best friend" for good reason.
2. Scuba diving can be dangerous.
3. Some hobbies can become businesses.
4. Poor or rude service can ruin a meal even in the finest restaurants.
5. Many people have little or no sense of time.

_____

_____

_____

_____

_____

35.1 Paragraphs That Follow the Order of Events

Use chronological order to present clearly the unfolding of an event or the steps in a process.

USES OF CHRONOLOGICAL ORDER
1. To explain how to do or make something 2. To tell about an incident 3. To organize details by time

EXERCISE A: Arranging Sentences in Chronological Order. Each group below contains a topic sentence and five supporting sentences. Number the supporting sentences so they can be written in chronological order.

EXAMPLE: Candy bars are less than one hundred years old.
a. M & M's, first introduced in 1940, were made for soldiers going off to World War II. __4__
b. In 1921, Baby Ruth bars appeared, but they were named for President Grover Cleveland's daughter, not for Babe Ruth. __3__
c. The first paper-wrapped candy, the Tootsie Roll, appeared in 1886. __2__
d. The very first candy bar was the Hershey Bar, first made in 1884. __1__
e. With the hard candy coating, the soldiers could get quick energy without getting sticky. __5__

1. Our day at the beach was a great success.

   a. My little brother was tired and slept all the way home. _____

   b. Few people were there, so we picked a choice spot near the water. _____

   c. We packed a picnic lunch. _____

   d. We got ice cream cones from a stand for dessert. _____

   e. The sandwiches tasted good, but a little sandy. _____

2. Some fruits have a long history, while others are more recent discoveries.

   a. The grapefruit has only been known for about three hundred years. _____

   b. Watermelons were grown in central Africa as far back as 2000 B.C. _____

   c. Apples were cultivated in Egypt in the 13th century B.C. _____

   d. Oranges are described in Chinese texts dating from 2200 B.C. _____

   e. The pineapple was discovered on the Caribbean island of Guadeloupe in 1493. _____

EXERCISE B: Writing a Paragraph with Chronological Order. Choose one of the groups from Exercise A. Use it to write a paragraph in chronological order that includes at least two transitions. You may change the wording a bit if it makes the transition smoother. Write your paragraph on a separate sheet of paper.

EXAMPLE: Candy bars are less than one hundred years old. The very first candy bar was the Hershey Bar, first made in 1884. Two years later, the first paper-wrapped candy, the Tootsie Roll, appeared. Nearly four decades later, in 1921, Baby Ruth bars appeared, but they were named for President Grover Cleveland's daughter, not for Babe Ruth. M & M's, first introduced in 1940, were made for soldiers going off to World War II. With the hard candy coating, the soldiers could get quick energy without getting sticky.

35.2 Paragraphs That Follow Spatial Order

Use spatial order to present details according to their physical location.

Topic Sentence	Details in Spatial Order
My first task was to identify the parts of the computer.	Directly in front of me was the keyboard. The small screen behind it was the monitor. To my right was the disk drive. To the left was the printer.

EXERCISE A: Arranging Sentences in Spatial Order. Each group below contains a topic sentence and four supporting sentences. Number the supporting sentences so they could be written in good spatial order.

EXAMPLE: When Grandma asks me to get her something from her purse, I always groan inwardly.
- a. Rolls of tissues and huge banded stacks of supermarket coupons hide whatever lies beneath them. ___3___
- b. A lumpy make-up bag and a wallet bulging with grandchildren's pictures are somewhere near the top. ___2___
- c. Whatever it is she wants is always at the bottom. ___4___
- d. A look at the outside and the sheer weight of the purse are enough to suggest that this will be no easy task. ___1___

1. The box on Grandpa's desk is one of my earliest memories and one of my favorite things.

   a. Beneath this false bottom, he keeps the set of scrimshaw buttons his grandfather made while he was on a whaling ship. _____

   b. The inside is lined with green velvet. _____

   c. The outside is carved with whaling scenes. _____

   d. A hidden spring at the right rear releases what seems to be the bottom of the inside. _____

2. The candy store in the center of town hasn't changed in the last fifty years.

   a. Behind the counter is a vast assortment of pumps for syrup and freezer bins for ice cream. _____

   b. The floor has a checkerboard pattern of green and yellow tiles. _____

   c. The counter is smooth, white marble with irregular hollow curves worn down by years of elbows. _____

   d. Round backless stools with black seats are lined up in front of the counter like silent soldiers. _____

EXERCISE B: Writing a Paragraph with Spatial Order. Choose one of the groups from Exercise A. Use it to write a paragraph in spatial order. Write your paragraph on a separate sheet of paper.

EXAMPLE: When Grandma asks me to get her something from her purse, I always groan inwardly. A look at the outside and the sheer weight of the purse are enough to suggest that this will be no easy task. A lumpy make-up bag and a wallet bulging with grandchildren's pictures are somewhere near the top. Rolls of tissues and huge banded stacks of supermarket coupons hide whatever lies beneath them. Whatever it is she wants is always at the bottom.

35.3 Paragraphs That Follow Order of Importance

Use order of importance to arrange examples, details, or reasons from least important to most important.

ORDER OF IMPORTANCE	
Topic Sentence	I have three objections to smoking.
Least Important Idea	It is a costly habit.
More Important Idea	It offends others and pollutes their environment.
Most Important Idea	It damages the smoker's health.

EXERCISE A: Arranging Sentences in Order of Importance. Each group below contains a topic sentence and four supporting sentences. Number the supporting sentences so that they could be written in order of importance.

EXAMPLE: Summer school was a good experience in several ways.
   a. I really learned a lot in the courses I took. __4__
   b. The classes were less formal than regular school. __2__
   c. I met students from the other schools in town. __3__
   d. The building is air conditioned. __1__

1. The abandoned Market Place Mall is a menace to the community.

   a. The deteriorating structure poses hazards to passers-by. _____

   b. Littering, graffiti, and vandalism have made it an eyesore. _____

   c. Strange characters make people afraid to shop in the surrounding area. _____

   d. The increasing trash and garbage will soon attract rats and other health hazards. _____

2. Grandparents and grandchildren have a very special relationship.

   a. A grandparent is patient and understanding because he or she does not have the same responsibilities that a parent has. _____

   b. Grandchildren help keep grandparents young and interested in things. _____

   c. Grandparents offer a sense of permanence and continuity with the past. _____

   d. Because there are few sources of conflict, grandparents are likely to be very pleased with their grandchildren. _____

EXERCISE B: Writing a Paragraph with Order of Importance. Choose one of the groups from Exercise A. Use it to write a paragraph in which the sentences are arranged in the order of importance. Add transitions where they will be helpful. Write your paragraph on a separate piece of paper.

EXAMPLE: Summer school was a good experience in several ways. For one thing, the building is air conditioned. In addition, the classes were less formal than regular school. I met students from the other schools in town. Most important, though, I really learned a lot in the courses I took.

36.1–36.3 Writing Paragraphs

Prewriting

1. Write a topic on the line below. Be sure it's narrow enough for a single paragraph.

TOPIC: _____

2. Write the main idea that your readers will want to know about your topic.

MAIN IDEA: _____

3. Next, write a topic sentence that includes your main idea. Try out a few on a separate sheet of paper before writing one below.

TOPIC SENTENCE: _____

4. On a separate piece of paper, brainstorm for support. Ask yourself questions about your main idea. The answers will be your support.

5. Go over your list of support. Cross out any unnecessary or unrelated ideas. Add any new information that may be necessary.

6. Decide what order—chronological order, spatial order, or order of importance—will best support your topic sentence.

ORDER: _____

7. Number your support in the order you have chosen.

Writing

Use your topic sentence and ordered list of supporting information to write a first draft of your paragraph. Change the order of the ideas if necessary, and remove any unrelated ideas. Use transitions to link your ideas smoothly.

Revising

Write *yes* or *no* to each of these questions. Then rework your first draft to fix all the items marked *no*.

1. Does the main idea of the paragraph cover all the other ideas? _____

2. Have you used enough examples, details, or incidents to develop the topic sentence fully?

_____

3. Have you eliminated any generalizations or weak statements that should be replaced with specific information? _____

4. Are all the pieces of supporting information directly related to your topic sentence? _____

5. Have you used the clearest order for arranging your ideas? _____

6. Have you used enough transitions to help the reader follow your ideas? _____

7. Do you need to change any words or sentences to make your paragraph clearer or more lively? _____

After you have improved your paragraph by turning the *no*'s into *yes*'s, **proofread** it carefully. Check for errors in sentence structure, capitalization, punctuation, and spelling. If necessary, make a final copy and proofread it again.

37.1 Looking at Compositions

A composition is a group of paragraphs organized around a single main idea.

THE PARTS OF A COMPOSITION	
Part	**Function**
Title	It catches the reader's interest and gives a general idea of the topic.
Introduction: the first paragraph	It introduces the topic, may give background information, makes the reader want to read on, and states the main idea.
Body Paragraphs: the middle of the composition	They present information that supports the main idea in a logical order. Each usually focuses on one part of the main idea.
Conclusion: the last paragraph	It reminds the reader of the main idea and brings the composition to a close in a striking, memorable way.

EXERCISE A: Understanding an Essay. Carefully read the composition below. Then complete the questions that follow it.

(1) Nature has its own rhythms, and each season holds its own natural charms. As the appeal of one season begins to weaken, people begin to look forward to the natural changes and special occasions of the next. Department stores, however, have no respect for such natural rhythms. They seem determined to create artificial seasons of their own.

(2) The "seasonal" department in most large stores changes regularly, but its goods rarely match the season. As soon as the after-Christmas sales end, the area is immediately flooded with garden and pool items; and a skier hoping to replace a broken pole will simply have to wait another year. By the time July Fourth comes around, school supplies have invaded the area, and the Halloween costumes are in evidence by Labor Day. Most often, long before the haunting day itself, the costumes are moved into a sale area, and the Christmas shop and Santa's Village expand to fill as much space as possible.

(3) The clothing rotation is even more unnatural. By mid-January, summer clothing begins appearing under the name of "cruise wear"; and by Valentine's Day, only spring and summer clothing is available. But beware if you are planning to wait until after the Fourth of July to get a bargain in swimwear. By then, even as people swelter in high temperatures, parkas, turtlenecks, and ski pants are the order of the day.

(4) Try as we might to keep to the natural rhythms of the seasons, the plan-ahead approach of stores is a hard force to resist. For if we fail to respond, the item we need in season will be out of season by the time we try to buy it.

1. What is the main point of the essay? _____

2. Which paragraph is the introduction? _____

3. Underline the topic sentence.

4. What do the other sentences in the introduction do? _____

5. Which paragraph is the conclusion? _____

6. Which are the supporting paragraphs? _____

7. What kind of support is used? _____

8. What order is used in the supporting paragraphs? _____

9. Underline any words or ideas in the conclusion that remind the reader of the main idea.

10. What would be a good title for this composition? _____

37.2–37.4 | Writing a Composition

Prewriting

1. Choose a topic and write it on the line below. Be sure it is narrow enough.

TOPIC: _____

2. Next, describe what your readers may know and how they may feel about your topic.

READERS: _____

3. Now decide on your purpose for writing (to describe, to tell a story, etc.).

PURPOSE: _____

4. Next write a sentence that states the main idea of your composition. Try out several before writing one below.

MAIN IDEA: _____

5. On a separate piece of paper, brainstorm for supporting information.

6. Go over your list of support and group your ideas to begin forming body paragraphs. Cross out any ideas that do not belong. Add any new information that may be needed.

7. Now decide what order you will use for your composition.

ORDER: _____

8. On a separate piece of paper, outline the body of your composition.

9. On the same paper, jot down ideas for your introduction, conclusion, and title.

Writing

Use your outline and notes for the introduction and conclusion to write a first draft of your composition. Be sure to follow a logical order and use transitions to connect ideas.

Revising

Write *yes* or *no* to each of the following questions. Then rework your first draft to fix all the items marked *no*.

1. Have I chosen a good title? _____

2. Do the opening sentences catch the reader's attention? _____

3. Have I included needed background information? _____

4. Does the main idea fit the composition? _____

5. Is the main idea expressed clearly? _____

6. Are the body paragraphs in the best order? _____

7. Does each paragraph have a topic sentence? _____

8. Have I included enough, and strong enough, support? _____

9. Are all the ideas closely related to the topic of each paragraph? _____

10. Does the conclusion recall the main idea and tie the whole composition together? _____

After you have improved your composition by turning the *no*'s into *yes*'s, **proofread** carefully. Look for mistakes in grammar, usage, mechanics, and spelling. If necessary, make a final copy and proofread again.

WRITING PROCESS PAGE

38.1 Looking at Reports

A report uses information gathered from research to support an original main idea. A report should include a bibliography that lists the sources used in the report.

SAMPLE BIBLIOGRAPHY ENTRIES	
Book	Lane, Ferdinand C. *All About the Flowering World.* New York: Random House, Inc., 1956.
Encyclopedia Article	*The New Book of Knowledge.* 1970 ed. "Plants."

EXERCISE A: Thinking About Reports. Write an appropriate answer to each of the following questions.

EXAMPLE: What parts of a report are the same as the parts of a composition? *title, introduction, body paragraphs, conclusion*

1. How is the information in a report different from the information in a composition? _____
_____

2. Where is the main idea of a report usually stated? _____

3. Where is support found? _____

4. What is the purpose of a bibliography? _____

5. How are items in a bibliography arranged? _____

EXERCISE B: Preparing Bibliography Entries. Choose one of the broad topics listed below. Use the card catalog in your library to write bibliography entries of the kind called for. You may check the chart above or the one of sample bibliography entries in Chapter 38 of your text to see how to set up the entries. When you have written the entries, number them to follow alphabetical order.

Cape Cod	bird watching
the Incas	Thomas Jefferson
holiday customs	the Civil War

EXAMPLE: a book by one author
Peterson, Roger Tory. *A Field Guide to the Birds: Eastern Land and Water Birds.* Boston, Massachusetts: Houghton Mifflin Company, 1947.

1. a book by one author

_____

_____

2. an encyclopedia article

_____

_____

3. a book by two authors

_____

_____

38.2–38.4 | Writing a Report

Prewriting

Choose a topic that interests you and for which you can find at least three good sources of information.

TOPIC: _____

2. On file cards, make a complete bibliography listing for each source you plan to use.
3. On a separate piece of paper, make a list of questions about your topic that you will answer through your research.
4. Use your list of questions to focus on a main idea for your report.

MAIN IDEA: _____

5. On file cards, take complete notes that relate to the main idea and answer the questions you want to answer.
6. Read over your notes and decide what subtopics you will use.

SUBTOPICS: _____

_____

7. Decide on a logical order for presenting the subtopics.

ORDER: _____

8. On separate paper, write a simple outline showing the organization of your subtopics and the supporting information.
9. Arrange your note cards to follow the order of your outline.
10. On the paper with your outline, jot down some ideas for your introduction, conclusion, and title.

Writing

Use your outline and note cards to write a first draft of your report on separate paper. If you use the exact words of a source or rephrase an author's idea, you will need to give the author, title, and page number in parentheses. Write your bibliography on a separate page.

Revising

Write *yes* or *no* to answer each of the following questions. Then rework your report to fix all the items marked *no*.

1. Is the title interesting and appropriate? _____
2. Does your introduction catch the reader's attention? _____
3. Does the introduction include all necessary background information? _____
4. Is the main idea stated in the best possible way? _____
5. Does your main idea have enough support? _____
6. Is all the information related to the main idea? _____
7. Are the subtopics in the best possible order? _____
8. Does each body paragraph have a topic sentence and enough support? _____
9. Is each body paragraph in the best possible order? _____
10. Do transitions connect sentences and paragraphs smoothly? _____
11. Have you credited all quotations, original ideas, and specific facts? _____
12. Does the conclusion recall the main idea in different words? _____
13. Is the bibliography complete, in the correct form, and in alphabetical order?

After you have improved your writing, **proofread** your report carefully, looking for errors in grammar, spelling, and mechanics. If necessary, make a final copy and proofread it again.

39.1 Looking at Book Reports

A book report tells readers what a book is about and whether they are likely to enjoy it.

BASIC PARTS OF A BOOK REPORT	
Part	**Function**
Introduction	Gives basic information, including title, author, kind of book, and a short summary, in one paragraph.
Body Paragraphs	Cover interesting features of the book, such as character, setting, and an important incident.
Conclusion	Offers an opinion about the book in one short paragraph.

EXERCISE A: Understanding a Book Report. Carefully read the brief book report below. Then complete the activities that follow.

(1) *Harriet Tubman: Conductor on the Underground Railroad,* by Ann Petry, is a biography of the runaway slave who helped hundreds escape to freedom. The Underground Railroad was neither under ground nor a railroad; but those who led the slaves to freedom were called conductors, and the houses where they were hidden were called stations.

The background of slavery in the years before the Civil War dominates the book. The fear of capture often overtook both conductors and passengers, for their owners would make their lives even worse than before. The runaways walked only under cover of darkness and hid in the woods, brush, and haystacks by day. Listening for the snap of a twig or any other sound that could signal the approach of a stranger, they slept little, constantly afraid of discovery. Even the stations where sympathetic strangers hid the runaways were sometimes checked by slave hunters.

Only a woman of Harriet Tubman's remarkable courage and unquenchable thirst for freedom could have accomplished what she did. Traveling most of the way on foot, she made over a dozen round trips between Maryland's Eastern Shore and what is now Ontario, Canada, leading her people to freedom. She inspired them when they were discouraged, urged them on when they were tired, prayed and sang with them to give them hope, and watched over them during their restless sleep. Harriet Tubman did whatever was necessary to get her passengers to safety. When necessary, she even threatened those who wanted to return to their owners, for she knew that they would be forced to reveal the routes and the stations where they had been. In all her journeys she never lost a single passenger and helped more than three hundred slaves to freedom.

1. What kind of book did the writer read? _____

2. What two features of the book does the writer focus on?

   _____   _____

3. Besides giving the title, author, and kind of book, what does the introduction discuss? _____

   _____

4. What part of the book report is missing? _____

5. How do you think the writer felt about the book? _____

EXERCISE B: Writing a Conclusion for a Book Report. Write a conclusion for the book report above. Give a favorable opinion about the book.

_____

_____

_____

39.2-39.4 Writing a Book Report

Prewriting

1. Choose a book you have read recently. Identify it in the spaces below.

TITLE: _____

AUTHOR: _____

2. Decide which features of the book you want to discuss.

FEATURES: _____

4. On separate paper, write down supporting information for each feature.
5. Arrange supporting information in each paragraph in logical order, and decide on the order of the body paragraphs.
6. Next outline the whole report. Jot down ideas for the introduction and conclusion.

Writing

Use your outline and list of supporting information to write a first draft of your book report. Be sure your report includes enough related information. Connect your ideas with transitions. If you quote from the book, be sure to use quotation marks and include page numbers in parentheses.

Revising

Write *yes* or *no* to each of the following questions. Then rework your first draft to fix all the items marked *no*.

1. Does the introduction include the author, title, and kind of book? _____
2. Does the introduction contain enough information about the content of the book? _____
3. Is there enough supporting information for each of the features of the book discussed? _____
4. Has all unnecessary information been eliminated? _____
5. Does every paragraph have a good topic sentence? _____
6. Are the ideas arranged in the most logical order? _____
7. Are all quotations in quotation marks? _____
8. Have you supplied page numbers for quotations? _____
9. Is the same tense used consistently throughout the report? _____
10. Is your recommendation supported with reasons?

After you have improved your book report by turning the *no*'s into *yes*'s, **proofread** carefully. Look for errors in grammar, mechanics, and spelling. If necessary, make a final copy and proofread it again.

WRITING PROCESS PAGE

40.1 Understanding Journals

A journal is a continuing record of a person's experiences.

CHARACTERISTICS OF JOURNAL ENTRIES	
Time of writing	Daily to a few times a week; often dated
Length	A few phrases to several pages
Readers	The writer alone or other readers
Content	Details about people, places, events, experiences; the writer's feelings

EXERCISE A: Examining a Journal Entry. Read carefully the journal entries below. Then answer the questions that follow them.

Friday, April 3. We had tryouts for the school play this afternoon, and I tried out for the part of the butler. I have no idea how I did because I was so nervous. I was really tired, too, because I was too nervous to sleep much last night. I picked a good scene, though, and at least I didn't mess up too much. It's going to be a long weekend, because we won't know the cast until Monday.

Monday, April 6. Hooray! I got it! The rehearsal schedule is pretty rough, so I'll have to work really hard to keep my grades up and still handle the play. But it'll be worth it!

1. What event does the writer record? _____

2. Do the entries reflect the writer's thoughts or feelings, or do they just record facts? _____

3. How regularly do you think the writer writes in his journal? _____

4. Are the two entries related in any way? Explain. _____

   _____

5. Whom do you think the writer intends to read his journal?

   _____

EXERCISE B: More Work with Journal Entries. Read the entries below. Then compare this journal with the one above.

Thursday, May 20. This problem with Sandy is really getting me down. How can she treat me this way when we've been friends since first grade? Today she promised to have lunch with me, and then Jeff came along and off she went with him. Then when we were getting ready to walk home together, she said, "See ya," and off she went with Mindy and Pam to meet Jeff, Ben, and Kevin. Then tonight she called as if nothing had ever happened and chattered away about mean old Mrs. Parkham and the report we have to write. I just don't understand her.

Friday, May 21. I've really had it with her! All week I've been counting on having Sandy stay over tonight. We were going to watch a TV movie and listen to records. At 5:00 she calls and says she's got this really scratchy throat and her mom won't let her come. But when I was sitting in the living room about half an hour ago, I saw her walking by with Jeff and Mindy. Till now, she's always been my best friend and I don't think she ever will be again, and I miss her.

_____

_____

_____

40.2 Keeping a Journal

When writing a journal, write about your own experiences; include your thoughts and feelings; and follow chronological order.

PLANNING A JOURNAL

1. Decide whether you will record daily experiences or only important events and whether you will be more concerned with ideas and feelings or only with what happens.
2. Decide how often you will write in your journal.
3. Decide on the kind of book you will use.
4. Decide whether your journal will be private or whether you will share it with others.

EXERCISE A: Planning a Journal Entry. Select an experience you have had in the last week. Answer these questions as preparation for writing a journal entry about the experience.

1. Who was involved in the experience? _____

2. What was the experience? _____

_____

3. When did it happen? _____

4. Where did it happen? _____

5. Why did it happen? _____

EXERCISE B: Writing a Journal Entry. Use the answers to the questions above to write a journal entry. Add details to make the experience more vivid. If you wish, include your ideas and feelings as well.

_____
_____
_____
_____
_____
_____
_____
_____
_____
_____
_____
_____
_____
_____
_____
_____
_____
_____
_____

41.1 Looking at Stories

A story usually has a main character, other characters, a setting, a conflict, a plot, and a narrator.

FEATURES OF STORIES

Main Character	The most important person in the story
Other Characters	Persons in the story who may be either helping or working against the main character
Setting	The time and location of the story
Conflict	A problem faced by the main character
Plot	Order of incidents in the story, usually leading to one main incident, the climax, when the conflict is settled
Narrator	The person telling the story: either a first-person narrator (a character in the story) or a third-person narrator (someone outside the story)

EXERCISE A: Recognizing Features of a Story. Identify each item below as (1) character, (2) setting, (3) plot. Then identify the narrator as (a) first person or (b) third person.

EXAMPLE: We plodded through the huge drifts and swirling snow toward the light in the cabin ahead of us. __2, a__

1. I tried to overcome my nervousness as my turn approached. _____

2. Behind him rose the sheer cliffs and ahead lay the open sea. _____

3. In Carla's daydreams she always made herself the heroine. _____

4. If help did not come soon, we would surely die. _____

5. Jason knew he had made the wrong choice, but it was too late to turn back now. _____

EXERCISE B: Examining a Story. Read a story from a book or magazine. Then answer the following questions about it.

1. Who is the main character? _____

2. What is the time of the action? _____

3. What is the location of the action? _____

4. What is the conflict? _____

5. Does the story have a first- or third-person narrator? _____

41.2-41.4 Writing a Story

Prewriting

1. Choose a main character for your story.

| MAIN CHARACTER: | _____ |

2. On a separate piece of paper, list details to make your character more real.
3. Describe the conflict that the main character will face.

| CONFLICT: | _____ |

4. What choice will the main character have to make to resolve the conflict?

| CHOICE: | _____ |

5. On separate paper, write character sketches for the other characters in the story.
6. Now decide on the setting for your story.

| TIME: | _____ | LOCATION: | _____ |

7. Next decide what kind of narrator you will use.

| NARRATOR: | _____ |

8. On separate paper outline the plot of your story. Decide how much time it will cover, how many incidents it will have, and what the climax will be.
9. On your plot outline, indicate places where dialogue would make the characters or plot more lively.

Writing

Use your plot outline and character sketches to write a first draft of your story. Be sure to use transitions to link incidents. Then think of a title that hints at the conflict of the story.

Revising

Write *yes* or *no* to answer each question. Then rework your first draft to fix all the items marked *no*.

1. Does the title fit the story? _____
2. Does the story have a strong beginning that will catch the reader's interest? _____
3. Is the setting clear? _____
4. Can a reader form a clear picture of each character? _____
5. Do the characters' actions and thoughts show their personalities? _____
6. Is the dialogue natural and appropriate for each character? _____
7. Does the story move smoothly from incident to incident? _____
8. Do transitions make the time and place of each incident clear? _____
9. Is the ending clear and believable? _____
10. Is the same narrator used consistently throughout the story? _____

After you have improved your story by turning the *no*'s into *yes*'s, **proofread** carefully. Look for errors in grammar, mechanics, and spelling. If necessary, make a final copy and proofread again.

42.1 Writing Friendly Letters

EXERCISE A: Writing a Friendly Letter. Choose one of the reasons below (or make up one of your own) and write a letter to a friend or relative. Be sure to write each letter part in the right place.

Invite a friend to spend the weekend.   Thank a relative for a gift.
Tell a camp friend about school.   Cheer up a sick person.

EXERCISE B: Addressing an Envelope. In the space below, address an envelope to go with the letter you wrote above.

42.2 Writing Business Letters

The six parts of a business letter are (1) the heading, (2) the inside address, (3) the salutation, (4) the body, (5) the closing, and (6) the signature. When you write a business letter, follow the standards of business-letter writing.

STANDARDS OF BUSINESS-LETTER WRITING	
Be polite.	Use business stationery.
Follow correct letter form.	Be neat.
Be brief and direct.	Include all necessary information.

EXERCISE A: Thinking About Business Letters. Answer each question below.

1. What part does a business letter have that a friendly letter does not?

   _____

2. What information does this extra part contain? _____

3. Where is it placed? _____

4. What punctuation mark follows the salutation in a business letter? _____

5. Why is it important to be brief and direct in a business letter?

   _____

EXERCISE B: Writing a Business Letter. In the space below, write to obtain price information or to order tickets for an upcoming concert or play in your area. Be sure to use correct letter form and follow the standards for business-letter writing.

43.1 Understanding Essay Questions

Answer an essay question only when you know exactly what it says.

GUIDES FOR READING ESSAY QUESTIONS
1. Read the question straight through to get a general sense of what it says. 2. Reread the question to get a clear and exact sense of what it is asking for. Notice words like *how, compare, describe, explain, discuss,* and so on, that indicate the kind of information wanted. 3. Determine for yourself just what the question is asking you to do and check your ideas against the test question.

EXERCISE A: Reading Essay Questions. Read carefully each essay question below. Underline any words that give clues to the kind of information that the answer requires. Then write a brief description of how the question should be answered.

EXAMPLE: Explain in detail how the parts of the ear transmit sound waves to the brain.
   Name the parts of the ear and tell how sound moves from one to the other until it
   reaches the brain.

1. Define aerobic exercise and describe its importance to heart and lung function.

_____

2. Describe the setting of the book *Island of the Blue Dolphins* and discuss how it is important to the action of the story.

_____

3. List in order the events leading to the capture of the pirate ship and tell how each heightens the excitement of the story.

_____

4. Discuss at least two effects of the discovery of gold in California.

_____

5. Compare the dwellings and clothing of the Plains Indians with those of the Navajo.

_____

EXERCISE B: Developing Essay-Test Skills. Read the essay question below. Then read the answer that follows. Tell whether the student who wrote the essay seems to have read the question carefully. Explain your answer.

Why was Copernicus important?

  Copernicus was born in Poland in 1473. He studied in a Polish university. He also studied law and medicine in Italy. Near the end of his life, his book about astronomy was published. In it his new ideas about the universe were explained. In Copernicus's time, people believed that the earth was the center of the universe. Copernicus died in 1543, but his ideas lived on.

_____

_____

_____

43.2 Writing Your Answers

Work on an essay question in a systematic way.

GUIDES FOR ANSWERING ESSAY QUESTIONS

1. Brainstorm for and list the ideas and facts you will need to answer the question.
2. Arrange the ones you plan to use in a modified outline.
3. Write your answer following the outline.
4. Go over your answer for clarity and correctness in the writing. Make sure that you have actually answered the question.

EXERCISE A: Planning an Essay Answer. In the spaces below, brainstorm for ideas and facts and then prepare a modified outline to answer the following essay question. (Allow about 20 minutes for this exercise.)

> Compare newspapers and TV news broadcasts in their coverage of current major news stories. Discuss the advantages and disadvantages of each medium.

BRAINSTORMING   OUTLINE

EXERCISE B: Writing an Essay Answer. Use your ideas and outline to write an essay answer to the question in Exercise A. When you have finished writing, check your answer carefully for errors in grammar, mechanics, and spelling. Also be sure you have actually answered the question and have done so completely.

_____

_____

_____

_____

_____

_____

_____

_____

_____

_____

44.1 Using a Dictionary and Thesaurus to Increase Your Vocabulary

Look up in a dictionary any word whose meaning you do not know and cannot figure out. Use a thesaurus to find the exact word you need when you are writing.

USING A DICTIONARY AND A THESAURUS
1. Read with a dictionary nearby.
2. Look up in a dictionary any word whose meaning you do not know and cannot figure out.
3. Use a thesaurus when you are writing and cannot think of the word that expresses just what you want to say.
4. Use the thesaurus by looking up a word that is similar in meaning to the word you need but cannot think of.

EXERCISE A: Using a Dictionary. Look up each word in a dictionary and write its meaning.

EXAMPLE: intruder   _one that enters as an improper or unwanted element_

1. illusion _____

2. morass _____

3. dilatory _____

4. intrepid _____

5. flagrant _____

6. culmination _____

7. restrain _____

8. stringent _____

9. acerbic _____

10. dexterity _____

EXERCISE B: Using a Thesaurus. Look up in a thesaurus each word in Exercise A, above, and write three words with a similar meaning for each.

EXAMPLE: inflammable—combustible, burnable, ignitable

1. _____

2. _____

3. _____

4. _____

5. _____

6. _____

7. _____

8. _____

9. _____

10. _____

44.2 Recognizing Synonyms, Antonyms, and Homonyms

Synonyms are words that are similar in meaning. Antonyms are groups of words that are opposite in meaning. Homonyms are words that sound alike but have different meanings and different spellings.

SYNONYMS, ANTONYMS, AND HOMONYMS		
Kind of Word	**Examples**	
Synonyms (words with similar meanings)	sum/total	cautious/careful
Antonyms (words with opposite meanings)	add/subtract	greeting/farewell
Homonyms (words that sound alike but	for, four, fore	
have different meanings and spellings)	pedal/peddle/petal	
	insight/incite	

EXERCISE A: Recognizing Synonyms, Antonyms, and Homonyms. Label each pair of words below as synonyms, antonyms, or homonyms.

EXAMPLE: threw, through ___*homonyms*___

1. dense, dents _____

2. past, future _____

3. appal, horrify _____

4. start, initiate _____

5. scene, seen _____

6. rouse, soothe _____

7. roomer, rumor _____

8. select, choose _____

9. entrance, exit _____

10. tactful, diplomatic _____

EXERCISE B: Writing Synonyms, Antonyms, and Homonyms. In the appropriate column below, write a synonym, antonym, and homonym for each word given.

EXAMPLE:	Synonym	Antonym	Homonym
to	*toward*	*from*	*too*
1. tense			
2. allowed			
3. peace			
4. ascent			
5. coarse			
6. plain			
7. great			
8. bold			
9. die			
10. pain			

44.3 Remembering the New Words You Learn

Record in a vocabulary notebook each new word that you learn.

SETTING UP A VOCABULARY NOTEBOOK		
Words	**Definitions**	**Examples**
serene	peaceful	The sleeping baby had a serene expression on his face.
humerus	a bone between the elbow and the shoulder	There is nothing humorous about a broken humerus.

EXERCISE A: Working with Vocabulary Words. In a dictionary, look up each word below. Then write its meaning and a sentence to help you remember it.

EXAMPLE: dilatory   _tending to delay   Tim's dilatory habits always result in his cramming for every test._

1. acrophobia _____

_____

2. infamous _____

_____

3. emaciated _____

_____

4. monologue _____

_____

5. copious _____

_____

6. tureen _____

_____

7. tundra _____

_____

8. ideogram _____

_____

9. effigy _____

_____

10. monetary _____

_____

EXERCISE B: More Work with Vocabulary Words. Read the following paragraph. Then use a dictionary to find the meaning of each underlined word. Write the word, its meaning, and an example sentence in your vocabulary notebook.

   Although many exercises are healthful, <u>aerobic</u> exercises are most frequently recommended by doctors. These are exercises that increase <u>cardiovascular</u> efficiency. Aerobic exercisers, though, should take care not to raise the <u>pulse</u> excessively and should obtain a doctor's advice on the best pulse rate for them. Those doing aerobics should check their pulse either at the <u>carotid</u> artery or at the <u>radial</u> artery regularly while exercising.

45.1 Seeing Words in Their Contexts

When you think about the meaning of a word, think about the context in which it is used.

CONTEXT
1. Context is the words and sentences that surround a word. 2. In ordinary speech and writing, every word has a context. 3. The context helps determine a word's meaning. 4. To understand what you read or hear, you may often have to think about the context in which a word is used.

EXERCISE A: Using Context to Learn Meaning. Write a short definition for the underlined word in each sentence.

EXAMPLE: Mom asked me to <u>mind</u> the baby for a few minutes. _____take care of_____

1. The funniest <u>sketch</u> poked fun at teen-age fashions. _____

2. A pawn is missing from the chess <u>set</u>. _____

3. A speck of <u>foreign</u> matter can make food unsafe. _____

4. Technical <u>terms</u> are explained in the glossary. _____

5. To draw a perfect circle, you need a <u>compass</u>. _____

6. After days of rain, the weather suddenly turned <u>fair</u>. _____

7. Dad is <u>presently</u> working at home. _____

8. No one wanted to speak in <u>defense</u> of censorship. _____

9. Finding her lost dog, Ann gave him a <u>fond</u> hug. _____

10. The Soviet Union <u>produces</u> large amounts of oil. _____

EXERCISE B: More Work with Context Clues. Use context clues to help you circle the letter of the correct meaning of each underlined word.

EXAMPLE: The flower market was a <u>riot</u> of bright colors. (a) noisy disorder (b) vivid display (c) comic scene (d) too much growth

1. Her friends <u>egged</u> Michelle on to enter the contest. (a) urged (b) discouraged (c) decorated (d) ridiculed

2. The <u>spell</u> was broken and the frog became a prince again. (a) period of time (b) spelling contest (c) kind of weather (d) words with magic power

3. Dad hired a boy to <u>prune</u> the overgrown hedges. (a) pick plums (b) uproot (c) trim (d) fence in

4. The playroom was a <u>sight</u> after the small children left it. (a) vision (b) something dreadful to see (c) something wonderful to see (d) glimpse

5. By the tenth round, it began to look as though the champ had met his <u>match</u>. (a) equal (b) inferior (c) future wife (d) conqueror

45.2 Using Context Clues to Find Word Meanings

Use context clues to figure out the meaning of a new word.

USING CONTEXT CLUES
1. Read the sentence carefully, and focus on it meaning.
2. Look for clues in nearby words.
3. Guess the meaning of the problem word.
4. Reread the sentence, seeing if the guessed meaning fits.
5. If possible, check a dictionary.

EXERCISE A: Identifying Context Clues. Write the meaning of each underlined word as it is suggested by its context. Underline words that are the most useful context clues.

EXAMPLE: In a famine, many people die of hunger. _____food shortage_____

1. As new areas became settled, pioneers pushed the frontier further into the wilderness. _____

2. Exposure to extreme heat can dry up the body's fluids, leaving a person dehydrated. _____

3. Petty thieves often became outcasts who were shunned by ordinary people. _____

4. The note was so illegible that no one could make it out. _____

5. Jill stepped from the sidewalk up onto the stoop and rang the doorbell. _____

6. A gardener with surplus tomatoes may give the unneeded ones away. _____

7. Strenuous activity, like running or fast swimming, speeds up the heartbeat. _____

8. Misdemeanors like littering or jaywalking usually receive light punishment. _____

9. This particular stamp has quite a history. _____

10. The boisterous party guests next door kept us awake for hours. _____

EXERCISE B: Using Context Clues. Use context clues to help you circle the letter of the correct meaning for each underlined word.

EXAMPLE: People convicted of felonies like robbery or arson may lose the right to vote.   (a) petty crimes (b) serious crimes   (c) misdemeanors   (d) treasonous acts

1. Many insecticides are also toxic to fish and animals.   (a) harmless   (b) poisonous (c) attractive   (d) beneficial

2. We found life in the country very different from urban life.   (a) of cities   (b) luxurious   (c) in the past   (d) rural

3. A good reporter should verify the facts he or she reports.   (a) check the correctness of   (b) rely on   (c) disprove   (d) doubt

4. Sandy soil is porous and allows water to drain off rapidly.   (a) allowing the passage of water (b) resisting the passage of water   (c) unproductive   (d) fertile

5. The poor clerk dreamed of buying his wife diamonds, furs, and other extravagant gifts. (a) unwisely expensive   (b) thoughtful   (c) practical   (d) sensible

46.1 Using Prefixes to Find Word Meanings

Use your knowledge of prefixes to figure out the meanings of unfamiliar words.

SEVEN COMMON PREFIXES		
Prefixes	**Meanings**	**Examples**
anti-	against	antitoxin — acting against a poison
mis-	wrong	misunderstand — understand wrongly
non-	not	nonreturnable — not returnable
pre-	before	predetermine — determine beforehand
re-	back, again	review — view again
semi-	half, partly	semicolon — half a colon
trans-	over, across	transpolar — across the polar region

EXERCISE A: Working with Prefixes. Use the prefixes above to help you write the meaning of the underlined word in each sentence.

EXAMPLE: Accepting only an occasional consulting job, Grandpa is now semiretired.
_____partly retired_____

1. Those who got a perfect score on the pretest did not have to complete the entire unit. _____

2. The transcontinental flight took only five hours. _____

3. Dad hopes to revisit the town where he grew up. _____

4. Angie prefers semiclassical music to rock. _____

5. We apologized for having misjudged Tom. _____

6. Workers in the antipoverty program are looking for affordable properties to convert to apartments.

_____

7. Biography is only one form of nonfiction. _____

8. Once it had been refinished, the table looked like new. _____

9. That anticancer medication has some harmful side effects. _____

10. The contractor used a nonstandard grade of lumber for parts of the deck. _____

EXERCISE B: More Work with Prefixes. Follow the directions for Exercise A, above.

1. Not long ago, transoceanic telephone calls were impossible. _____

2. Mom had antifreeze put in the car when the oil was changed. _____

3. The police will reopen the investigation because of new information. _____

4. Most one-year-olds utter mainly nonsense syllables. _____

5. Many congressional leaders felt that the President's actions were a misuse of power. _____

6. Lincoln's antislavery stand in the debates with Stephen Douglass gained him national recognition.

_____

7. Although common elsewhere, mimosa trees are almost nonexistent in this region. _____

8. Marci misdealt the cards and had to deal again. _____

9. Be sure to use only semisweet chocolate in this recipe. _____

10. Derek will not be readmitted to school without a written note from his doctor. _____

46.2 Using Suffixes to Find Word Meanings

Use your knowledge of suffixes to figure out the meanings of unfamiliar words.

SEVEN COMMON SUFFIXES		
Suffixes	**Meanings**	**Examples**
-able (or -ible)	capable of being	changeable
-ism	idea, belief, act	realism
-ist	believer, doer	perfectionist
-less	without	childless
-ly	in a certain way	naturally
-ment	a result, act, fact, condition	requirement
-tion (or -ion or -sion)	the act of, the state of being	attraction

EXERCISE A: Working with Suffixes. Use the suffixes above to help you write the meaning of the underlined word in each sentence.

EXAMPLE: His rough <u>treatment</u> of the kitten shocked us.   _act of treating_

1. That soft drink comes only in <u>returnable</u> bottles. _____

2. The doctor called the patient's condition <u>hopeless</u>. _____

3. The <u>cyclist</u> trained hard for the big race. _____

4. Most birds follow the same pattern of <u>migration</u> each year. _____

5. Many people find it hard to accept <u>criticism</u>. _____

6. Joe found his <u>confinement</u> to the house the hardest part of his recovery. _____

7. The rain stopped as <u>suddenly</u> as it had started. _____

8. Many cities lack enough <u>affordable</u> housing. _____

9. The jeweler said that the ring was <u>worthless</u>. _____

10. The <u>vibration</u> of the old engine made the whole car shake. _____

EXERCISE B: More Work with Suffixes. Follow the directions for Exercise A.

1. That is not a <u>desirable</u> location for a shopping mall. _____

2. Some people make fun of Darryl's <u>idealism</u>. _____

3. The <u>journalist</u> won an award for her investigation into the mayor's finances. _____

4. Kevin's comment was not deliberately cruel, just <u>thoughtless</u>. _____

5. Louise left the room <u>abruptly</u>. _____

6. This writing <u>assignment</u> is taking more time than I had planned. _____

7. The panel <u>discussion</u> ended with a question-and-answer period. _____

8. Dana <u>proudly</u> waved her report card in the air. _____

9. Some <u>resentment</u> between children in a family is normal. _____

10. That woman became famous as a <u>panelist</u> on a TV game show. _____

47.1 Looking into the Origins of Words

Loanwords are foreign-language words that have become a part of the English language.

ORIGINS OF SOME COMMON LOANWORDS

Dutch: cruller, cole slaw, stoop, sleigh
Spanish: lasso, corral, ranch, barbecue, avocado
French: prairie, rapids, chowder, depot
German: slim, ouch, wiener, kindergarten
American Indian: squash, papoose, totem, skunk

EXERCISE A: Exploring the Origins of Words. Using a dictionary that gives word origins, write the language from which each of the following words came into English.

EXAMPLE: croissant ___*French*___

1. pecan _____
2. tom-tom _____
3. moccasin _____
4. pumpernickel _____
5. graffiti _____
6. amen _____
7. smorgasbord _____
8. shillelagh _____
9. adobe _____
10. gumbo _____

EXERCISE B: More Work with Word Origins. Follow the directions for Exercise A, above.

1. kimono _____
2. matzoh _____
3. yam _____
4. toboggan _____
5. patio _____
6. matinee _____
7. kumquat _____
8. libretto _____
9. ballet _____
10. shish kebab _____

47.2 Exploring Changes in Language

Language changes by developing new words for new things and new meanings for old words.

New Words for New Things	New Meanings for Old Words
yuppie: young urban professional	*black box:* very complicated electronic equipment
quark: particle of matter much smaller than an atom	*scenario:* originally an outline for a play; now a series of events, proposed or imagined

EXERCISE A: Learning New Meanings of Old words. Look up the following words in a recent dictionary. Write the meaning that you think is most recent.

EXAMPLE: language   *a set of symbols and rules used in computers*

1. chip _____

_____

2. terminal _____

_____

3. memory _____

_____

4. debug _____

_____

5. display _____

_____

EXERCISE B: Learning the Meanings of New Words for New Things. Look up the following words in a recent dictionary and write their meanings.

EXAMPLE: interferon   *substance produced by the body to fight viruses*

1. modem _____

_____

2. burnout _____

_____

3. bionics _____

_____

4. aerobics _____

_____

5. hydrofoil _____

_____

48.1 Using a Dictionary to Check Your Spelling

Look up any word whose spelling you are unsure of.

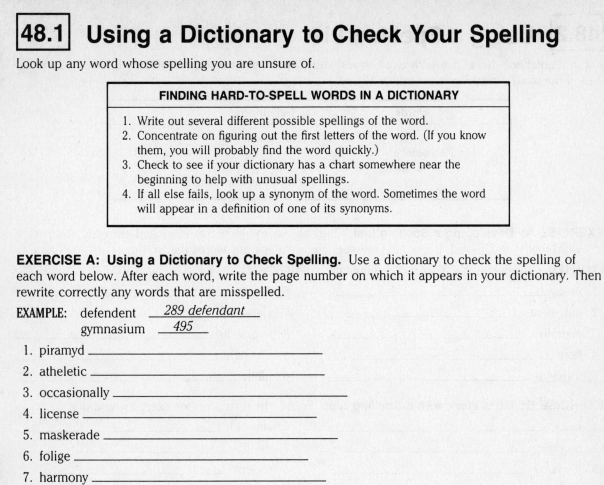

FINDING HARD-TO-SPELL WORDS IN A DICTIONARY
1. Write out several different possible spellings of the word. 2. Concentrate on figuring out the first letters of the word. (If you know them, you will probably find the word quickly.) 3. Check to see if your dictionary has a chart somewhere near the beginning to help with unusual spellings. 4. If all else fails, look up a synonym of the word. Sometimes the word will appear in a definition of one of its synonyms.

EXERCISE A: Using a Dictionary to Check Spelling. Use a dictionary to check the spelling of each word below. After each word, write the page number on which it appears in your dictionary. Then rewrite correctly any words that are misspelled.

EXAMPLE: defendent ____*289 defendant*____
gymnasium ____*495*____

1. piramyd _____
2. atheletic _____
3. occasionally _____
4. license _____
5. maskerade _____
6. folige _____
7. harmony _____
8. fourty _____
9. heighth _____
10. breadth _____

EXERCISE B: More Work Checking Spelling. Follow the directions for Exercise A, above.

1. vegtable _____
2. honorery _____
3. inquisition _____
4. discouraging _____
5. independance _____
6. presence _____
7. elementry _____
8. corrugated _____
9. imaginery _____
10. ridgid _____

48.2 Using a Spelling List

List in a notebook those frequently used words whose spellings give you trouble. Include definitions as well, if the word's meaning is unfamiliar to you.

Words	Definitions
aggravate	to make worse
definite	
ridiculous	
psyche	soul, spirit, or mind

EXERCISE A: Developing a Spelling List. Copy any word below that is spelled correctly. Rewrite any word that is misspelled. Record in your spelling notebook any words that you miss.

EXAMPLES: deceive _deceive_   illiminate _eliminate_

1. usualy _____
2. judgment _____
3. genralize _____
4. fiery _____
5. tornadoe _____

6. discriptive _____
7. vigilence _____
8. ungrateful _____
9. copiright _____
10. ninth _____

EXERCISE B: More Work with a Spelling List. Follow the directions for Exercise A, above.

1. neice _____
2. drudgery _____
3. jeopardy _____
4. parralell _____
5. reverce _____

6. sensable _____
7. frontier _____
8. reciept _____
9. rinoceros _____
11. porcupine _____

NAME _____ CLASS _____ DATE _____

49.1 Forming Plurals

To form the plurals of most nouns, add -s or -es. Learn those few nouns that form their plurals irregularly.

FORMING PLURALS

1. Simply add -s to form the plural of most nouns. *(homes, artists, places)*
2. When a noun ends in -s, -ss, -x, -z, -sh, or -ch, add -es to form the plural. *(buses, glasses, boxes, fizzes, wishes, birches)*
3. When a word ends in a consonant plus -y, change y to i and add -es. *(gravies, babies)*
4. When a word ends in -fe, change f to v and add -es. *(knives)*
5. When a word ends in a consonant plus -o, add -es. *(torpedoes)* Exceptions: musical terms and words from other languages— *solos, ponchos*

EXERCISE A: Writing Plurals. Write the plural form of each of the following nouns.

EXAMPLE: belief ___*beliefs*___

1. zero _____
2. library _____
3. mess _____
4. shark _____
5. alto _____
6. butterfly _____
7. pencil _____
8. marsh _____
9. ox _____
10. whiz _____
11. tax _____
12. march _____
13. memory _____
14. foot _____
15. radio _____
16. football _____
17. class _____
18. child _____
19. attorney _____
20. clam _____

EXERCISE B: More Work with Plurals. Each noun below has a spelling change from singular to plural. Write each missing form to complete the chart.

EXAMPLE: Singular   Plural
              worry   worries

Singular	Plural
1. mouse	_____
2. _____	wives
3. cry	_____
4. _____	women
5. _____	directories
6. gooseberry	_____
7. _____	lice
8. man	_____
9. story	_____
10. life	_____

49.2 Adding Prefixes to Words

When a prefix is added at the beginning of a word, the spelling of that word stays the same.

WORDS BEGINNING WITH PREFIXES	
cooperative	co- + operative
deform	de- + form
disappear	dis- + appear
immature	im- + mature
independent	in- + dependent
mismanagement	mis- + management
reexplore	re- + explore
unnecessary	un- + necessary

EXERCISE A: Spelling Words with Prefixes. Correctly write a new word for each word below by adding the prefix given in parentheses.

EXAMPLE: material (im-) *immaterial*

1. ordinate (co-) _____

2. value (de-) _____

3. service (dis-) _____

4. print (im-) _____

5. operative (in-) _____

6. speak (mis-) _____

7. educate (re-) _____

8. noticeable (un-) _____

9. anchor (co-) _____

10. moralize (de-) _____

EXERCISE B: More Work with Prefixes. Follow the directions for Exercise A, above.

1. exist (co-) _____

2. frost (de-) _____

3. enchant (dis-) _____

4. mortal (im-) _____

5. use (mis-) _____

6. establish (re-) _____

7. significant (in-) _____

8. neighborly (un-) _____

9. star (co-) _____

10. compose (de-) _____

NAME _____ CLASS _____ DATE _____

49.3 Adding Suffixes to Words

When a suffix is added at the end of a word, the spelling of the word often changes.

SPELLING RULES FOR ADDING SUFFIXES

Rule 1. When a word ends in a consonant plus -y, change the y to i before adding a suffix. (happy, happiness) Exception: suffixes beginning with i (deny, denying)

Rule 2. When a word ends in a vowel plus -y, make no change before adding a suffix. (annoy, annoyance) Exceptions: day, daily; gay, gaily

Rule 3. When a word ends in -e, drop the e before adding a suffix beginning with a vowel. (promote, promotion) Exception: words ending in -ce or -ge (trace, traceable; courage, courageous)

Rule 4. When a word ends in -e, make no change before adding a suffix beginning with a consonant. Exceptions: true, truly; argue, argument; judge, judgment

Rule 5. When a one-syllable word ends in a single vowel plus a single consonant, double the final consonant before adding a suffix beginning with a vowel. (knit, knitting) Exceptions: words ending in x or w (tax, taxing; sew, sewing)

EXERCISE A: Spelling Words with Suffixes. Make a new word out of each word below by using the suffix given in parentheses. Be sure you spell the new word correctly.

EXAMPLE: busy (-ly) ___busily___

1. box (-er) _____   6. envy (-ous) _____
2. pry (-ed) _____   7. portray (-ed) _____
3. note (-able) _____   8. squeeze (-able) _____
4. nice (-ly) _____   9. whip (-ed) _____
5. grow (-ing) _____   10. merry (-ment) _____

EXERCISE B: More Work with Suffixes. Follow the directions for Exercise A, above.

1. rely (-ing) _____   6. trip (-ed) _____
2. employ (-able) _____   7. throw (-ing) _____
3. beauty (-ful) _____   8. create (-ion) _____
4. argue (-able) _____   9. pretty (-ly) _____
5. manage (-able) _____   10. array (-ed) _____

Copyright © by Prentice-Hall, Inc.

153

49.4 Choosing Between *ei* and *ie*

When a word has a long *e* sound, use *ie*. When a word has a long *a* sound, use *ei*. When a word has a long *e* sound preceded by the letter *c,* use *ei*.

SPELLING WORDS WITH *EI* AND *IE*			
Long e Sound	**Long a Sound**	**Long e After c**	**Exceptions**
relief	weight	receive	either seize
thief	neighborly	ceiling	neither friend

EXERCISE A: Spelling *ie* and *ei* Words. On the line after each sentence, write correctly the incomplete word within the sentence.

EXAMPLE: Many sea explorations occurred during the r __ __ gn of Queen Elizabeth I.
_____*reign*_____

1. The new family next door doesn't seem very fr __ __ ndly. _____
2. The wedding cake had several t __ __ rs. _____
3. The tiger looked especially f __ __ rce when it was hungry. _____
4. Someone left the telephone rec __ __ ver off the hook. _____
5. The f __ __ ld was dotted with wild flowers. _____
6. The geologists have discovered a new v __ __ n of ore. _____
7. The rider held the r __ __ ns too tightly. _____
8. The table is twenty inches in h __ __ ght. _____
9. I am Aunt Mary's only n __ __ ce. _____
10. We had trouble bel __ __ ving Jim's story. _____

EXERCISE B: More Work wih *ie* and *ei*. Follow the directions for Exercise A, above.

1. My brother is in __ __ ghth grade. _____
2. The two child-warriors used trash can lids as sh __ __ lds. _____
3. The old Parson farm has sl __ __ gh rides during the winter. _____
4. No passenger trains but only fr __ __ ght trains use those tracks. _____
5. I am sure __ __ ther Jake or Karen will be home. _____
6. The spaniel is b __ __ ge with white ears. _____
7. Everyone in the n __ __ ghborhood attended the block party. _____
8. The game was delayed br __ __ fly by the shower. _____
9. My brother lifts w __ __ ghts every day. _____
10. W __ __ rd moaning sounds came from the old abandoned house. _____

50.1 Setting Up a Study Area

Set up a study area where you can concentrate on your school work.

GUIDELINES FOR A GOOD STUDY AREA
Your study area should be the same every day. It should 1. Be comfortable 2. Be free of constant interruptions 3. Be off-limits to other people 4. Equipped with a desk or table and chair 5. Be well-lighted 6. Be equipped with all the tools needed for school work 7. Include a posted study schedule

Materials for a home study area should include the following:

pens and pencils	ruler
paper and notebooks	wastepaper basket
erasers	magic markers and crayons
tape	index cards
stapler and paper clips	manila folders
scissors	dictionary

EXERCISE A. Examining Your Study Area. Answer the following questions about your study area.

EXAMPLE: Describe the lighting of your study area ___*high-intensity desk lamp*___

1. Describe the lighting of your study area. _____
2. Describe the table or desk on which you study. _____
3. Do you have a comfortable chair? _____
4. Is your study area reasonably quiet? _____
5. Is your study area free of interruptions? _____
6. List features of your study that make it good for studying. _____
7. List any features that could be improved. _____
8. List the reference books kept in your study area. _____
9. What other books would be helpful to have there? _____
10. Do you have a work schedule posted? _____

EXERCISE B: Checking on Needed Equipment. Answer *Yes* or *No* to the following questions.

EXAMPLE: Does your study area have its own waste basket? ___*Yes*___

1. Is your study area equipped with pens and pencils? _____
2. Does it have a pencil sharpener? _____
3. Is it well supplied with paper, index cards, and folders? _____
4. Does it have a good recent dictionary? _____
5. Does it have a pair of scissors and a stapler? _____

50.2 Scheduling Study Time

Create a study schedule that you can follow every day. To draw up a study schedule, follow these directions.

SETTING UP A STUDY SCHEDULE

1. Divide time after school into half-hour segments.
2. Block out regularly scheduled after-school activities.
3. Block out your usual dinner hour.
4. Block out no more than one hour for television viewing.
5. Block out at least two hours for homework. Break this time into two separate segments.
6. Block out at least one half-hour before bed for pleasure reading.
7. Put your schedule on paper and attach it to your study area.

EXERCISE A: Evaluating Your Study Time. Answer the questions below about the most recent day during which you studied.

EXAMPLE: How many hours did you block out for studying? ___two hours___

1. How many hours did you block out for studying? _____

2. What subjects did you study? How much time for each? _____
_____

3. What was the most difficult material and how much time did you give it? _____
_____

4. Did you study as long as you had planned to? _____

5. Did you divide your total study time into segments? _____

6. How many segments did you divide your time into? How long was each? _____
_____

7. Were there any distractions? If so, what were they? _____
_____

8. Did you remain in your study area the whole time? _____

9. How much time did you spend viewing television? _____

10. Did you have time for any pleasure reading? How much? _____

EXERCISE B: Preparing a Study Schedule. Complete the following study schedule for an average school night.

Time	Activity	Time	Activity
3:30–4:00	after-school activities	6:00–6:30	_____
4:00–4:30	_____	6:30–7:00	_____
4:30–5:00	_____	7:00–7:30	_____
5:00–5:30	_____	7:30–8:00	_____
5:30–6:00	_____	8:00–8:30	_____

50.3 Finding Time to Read for Pleasure

Set aside time every day for pleasure reading.

SOURCES OF TIPS FOR GOOD READING
Librarians, who can recommend books on what interests you
Friends who read and who share your interests
Reading lists in school books and in libraries
Bookstores, where you can usually browse or get suggestions
TV programs on interesting subjects also treated in books

EXERCISE A: Planning Time for Pleasure Reading. In the appropriate blank, check the frequency with which you use each opportunity for pleasure reading.

	Often	Occasionally	Never
EXAMPLE: On the school bus	____	____✓	____
1. Before leaving for school	____	____	____
2. On the school bus	____	____	____
3. Free-reading time in school	____	____	____
4. During lunch period	____	____	____
5. At recess	____	____	____
6. Before dinner	____	____	____
7. While baby-sitting	____	____	____
8. At bedtime	____	____	____
9. Weekends	____	____	____
10. While riding in a car	____	____	____

EXERCISE B: Reviewing Sources of Reading Tips. List books you have read within the last year that were not assigned by a teacher. Tell what led you to read each one: the suggestion of a parent, or a librarian, teacher, or friend; reading a book review; the fact that you had read and liked another book by the same author; a suggestion made on a television program; some other reason.

EXAMPLE: *Blubber,* by Judy Blume—liked other book by Judy Blume

1.

2.

3.

4.

5.

51.1 Organizing a Notebook

Keep your notebook organized, complete, and neat.

HOW TO ORGANIZE A NOTEBOOK
1. Put plenty of looseleaf paper into your binder. 2. Use dividers to mark off sections for each subject. 3. Use gummed reinforcements around the paper holes. 4. Keep all notes in the same subject together. 5. Put in where they belong returned homework assignments and tests that may be useful for future studying. 6. Rewrite any notes that are sloppy or hard to read.

EXERCISE A: Evaluating Your Notebook. Rate your own notebook by putting a check in the appropriate space below.

EXAMPLE:	Usually	Occasionally	Rarely
Rewrite notes that are hard to read	_____	____✓____	_____
1. Keep plenty of paper in notebook	_____	_____	_____
2. Have section for each subject	_____	_____	_____
3. Use dividers to mark off sections	_____	_____	_____
4. Use gummed reinforcements to keep pages from falling out	_____	_____	_____
5. Insert notes on classes missed	_____	_____	_____
6. Insert homework and tests next to notes they relate to	_____	_____	_____
7. Rewrite notes that are hard to read	_____	_____	_____
8. Try to keep notes clear and readable	_____	_____	_____
9. Key mark important notes	_____	_____	_____
10. Use notes for reports and in studying for tests	_____	_____	_____

EXERCISE B: Improving Your Notebook. Choose five answers from Exercise A that show ways in which your notebook could be improved. List things you can do to improve on these areas.

EXAMPLE: Will try to rewrite all notes that are hard to read

1.

2.

3.

4.

5.

51.2 Making Modified Outlines

Use a modified outline to take notes on what you hear in class or read.

TIPS FOR MAKING MODIFIED OUTLINES
1. As you listen in class or read, ask yourself, "What is the subject I am hearing or reading about?"
2. A brief statement of the subject will be the heading of your outline.
3. Jot down details that contain useful information about the subject.

EXERCISE A: Completing a Modified Outline. Complete the modified outline below, supplying the missing items in the blanks. Draw the needed information from the paragraph.

Everyone values diamonds, but few know the basic facts about them. Diamonds are the hardest substance known, consisting of pure crystallized carbon. They come in many shapes. Some have eight sides, and some have as many as forty-eight. Purity of color is rare in diamonds because small imperfections, such as air bubbles, make them cloudy. In addition to the clear white most often seen in engagement rings, diamonds may be yellow, green, blue, or even brown. The largest and most nearly perfect of the blue-stone diamonds is the Hope diamond. It is worth a very large fortune.

1. Hardest substance known

2. _____

3. Come in many shapes

4. _____

5. _____

6. May be white, yellow, green, blue, brown

7. _____

EXERCISE B: Making a Modified Outline. On a separate sheet of paper, make a modified outline of the paragraph below.

Insects are small for a good reason. Unlike human beings and most animals, insects have no lungs to breathe with. Instead, tiny tubes carry air from the outside of the insect's body to all of the parts inside. These tubes do not work well over long distances, however. Therefore, if the insect grows too large, breathing becomes impossible.

51.3 Making Formal Outlines

Use formal outlines to summarize chapters of textbooks and to prepare for the writing of a report.

```
┌─────────────────────────────────────────────────────────┐
│              PATTERN FOR A FORMAL OUTLINE                 │
├─────────────────────────────────────────────────────────┤
│   I. First main idea                                     │
│      A. }                                                │
│      B. } Major details explaining I.                    │
│            1. }                                          │
│            2. } Minor details explaining B.             │
│   II. Second main idea                                   │
└─────────────────────────────────────────────────────────┘
```

EXERCISE A: Working with Formal Outlines. Use the facts on the left to complete the partial outline.

Indian names for states
Oklahoma—Choctaw word for "red people"
Ohio—Iroquois word for "good river"
Wyoming—means "large prairie place." Taken from name of Pennsylvania valley popularized in a poem and used to name new Western state
Spanish names for states
Colorado—means "red color"
Arizona—means "silver-bearing"
Montana—means "mountainous place"

Origins of State Names

I. Names of Indian Origin
  A. Oklahoma _____
  B. _____
  C. _____
     1. Name for part of Pennsylvania
     2. _____

II. _____
  A. _____
  B. Arizona _____
  C. Montana _____

EXERCISE B: Making a Formal Outline. On a separate sheet of paper, make a formal outline of the material in the three paragraphs below.

Money

Money has a long history. The earliest kinds do not seem much like our modern money. For example, the ancient Egyptians used grain for money. They stored it in huge warehouses. They could even write checks against the grain they had stored there. The Greeks used cattle as money for many centuries. People living on the islands of the Pacific used shells and rare stones.

The Chinese were the first people to mint coins. Their coins had pictures of tools on them. They had holes in the middle so that they could be strung together. Greek city states began to use coins in about the 8th century B.C. Alexander the Great introduced a uniform coinage system in all of the countries he conquered.

The invention of paper money can also be traced to the Chinese. They printed this money in blue ink on paper made from the bark of the mulberry tree. They called it "flying money" because it could be blown away by the wind. The first modern banknotes were used in England in the late 1600's.

52.1 Separating Fact from Opinion

A statement of fact can be proved true or false; a statement of opinion cannot be.

RECOGNIZING FACTS AND OPINIONS

1. A statement of fact can be tested by direct observation or measurement.
2. A statement of fact can be tested by an experiment.
3. A statement of fact can be tested by reference books or records.
4. A statement of fact can be tested by consulting an authority.
5. An opinion expresses a personal feeling, a judgment, or a prediction.

EXERCISE A: Identifying Facts and Opinions. Write *fact* or *opinion* on the line after each statement. Remember: A statement of fact may express what is false.

EXAMPLE: A mile consists of 10,000 feet. ___*fact*___

1. The red dress looks better on you than the green one. _____

2. It is pleasant to spend an afternoon at the beach. _____

3. That car costs over $10,000 dollars. _____

4. Next year, our team will finish no worse than second in the league. _____

5. William Blake wrote the poem "The Lamb." _____

6. "The Lamb" is twenty lines long. _____

7. "The Lamb" is thirty lines long. _____

8. My brother goes to an excellent college. _____

9. This tree cannot survive another storm. _____

10. A Civil War battle was once fought in this town. _____

EXERCISE B: More Work with Facts and Opinions. Write *fact* or *opinion* on the line after each statement.

EXAMPLE: This road will be repaired soon because there are many potholes in it. ___*opinion*___

1. Many doctors and medical experts have stated that smoking cigarettes is harmful to a person's health. _____

2. Jackie will grow up to be over six feet tall, because both his parents are very tall.

   _____

3. The bridge over the river is nearly half a mile long. _____

4. If you want to become a championship swimmer, you should start training before you are four years old. _____

5. Franklin Delano Roosevelt was America's greatest President, because he was elected President more times than anyone else. _____

52.2 Recognizing Uses of Language

Different words can have the same basic meaning but different tones, or emotional suggestions. The meaning of a statement is affected by the tone of the words and phrases used.

Favorable Tone	Neutral Tone	Unfavorable Tone
public servant	public official	politician
refuse	waste	garbage
indisposed	ill	sick
cuisine	food	chow

EXERCISE A: Identifying the Tone of Words. Tell whether the underlined words and phrases have a favorable or an unfavorable tone.

EXAMPLE: Charles is a real egghead. ___*unfavorable*___

1. What slop are you eating for lunch today? _____

2. Mr. Bellamy is one of our most distinguished senior citizens. _____

3. Mrs. Bell is a well-respected educator. _____

4. Mrs. Bell is a schoolmarm. _____

5. Did the garbage man come today? _____

6. The sanitation workers were here at 6:00 A.M. _____

7. The doctor said that I require a surgical procedure. _____

8. The doctor said I have to go under the knife. _____

9. As a bench warmer, Phil does not get into the game every day. _____

10. As a reserve player, I must be ready to play when called upon. _____

EXERCISE B: More Work with Word Tone. Choose the word with the more favorable tone and write it in the space provided.

EXAMPLE: The surgeon made a deep (cut, incision). ___*incision*___

1. Ronald is a good-looking (child, kid). _____

2. You seem very (excitable, high-spirited) today. _____

3. I have to take (pills, medication) every morning. _____

4. There seems to be a (mistake, miscalculation) in your arithmetic. _____

5. The skater's ankle still feels (tender, sore). _____

6. Donna is (fussy, careful) about her stamp collection. _____

7. "I'll sell you a terrific (used car, previously owned automobile)." _____

8. Mr. Prince formed an association of local (merchants, shopkeepers). _____

9. That apple looks (overripe, rotten). _____

10. Three workers were (terminated, fired) last week. _____

53.1 Reading Textbooks

Use the special features of your textbooks to improve your schoolwork.

SOME FEATURES OF TEXTBOOKS

1. The table of contents lists units and chapters and the pages on which each begins.
2. The index lists alphabetically all subjects covered in the book and the pages on which they are discussed. Located in the back of the book.
3. The glossary (also in the back of the book) defines special terms.
4. Chapter titles, headings, and subheadings are printed in large, heavy type. They tell you what you will be reading about and divide the material into manageable sections for study and review.
5. Questions and exercises at chapter end can be looked at before reading the chapter to preview its contents. Afterwards questions and exercises help you to review what you have learned.
6. Pictures and captions (information given next to or beneath a picture) can make explanations clearer and descriptions more vivid.
7. Summaries offer a quick review of what you have read and highlight main points.

EXERCISE A: Examining the Features in Your Textbook. Answer the following questions, using a textbook from another course.

1. How many headings are there in a typical chapter? _____

2. How many subheadings are there? _____

3. Does a reading of just headings and subheadings give you an outline of the chapter's content?

_____

4. Is there a chapter introduction? What seems to be its purpose? _____

5. How much can you learn about the contents of a chapter by examining chapter-end exercises and

questions before reading it? _____

6. Do chapters or units end with summaries? _____

7. Does the textbook have a glossary? _____

8. Compare the glossary entries with the same entries in a dictionary. How do the entries differ?

_____

9. Examine some pictures and their captions. Do they add any important content to the chapters in

which they are found? _____

10. Think of a major topic covered in the textbook. Which is the faster way of looking it up—using the

table of contents or the index? _____

EXERCISE B: Surveying Another Textbook. Use the questions of Exercise A in examining a textbook for a different course. Use a separate piece of paper for your answers.

53.2 Preparing for a Test

Do not rely on last-minute cramming to prepare for a test.

PREPARING FOR A TEST

1. Review your notes or textbook chapter three times: the evening of the day when you took the notes, two days later, and the night before a test.
2. To find out what you do not know, make up questions covering the material you will be tested on, and write out the answers. Problems that arise will tell you where you are weak.
3. To memorize things, go over them repeatedly for at least several days before a test, and ask someone to quiz you on the material. Do your memorization after your other homework.

EXERCISE A: Evaluating Your Test Preparation. Check up on your strong and weak points in test preparation by answering *Yes* or *No* to the following questions.

EXAMPLE: Do you review your notes the night before a test? ___*Yes*___

1. Do you use your notebook notes to get ready for a test? _____
2. Do you review your notes on the evening of the day you take them? _____
3. Do you review the same notes two days later? _____
4. Do you review these notes the night before a test? _____
5. Do you make up questions on the material the test will cover? _____
6. Do you write out the answers to these questions? _____
7. If you run into problems, do you look for needed information? _____
8. Do you go over material to be memorized repeatedly for several days before a test? _____
9. Do you do your memorizing as the last part of your homework? _____
10. Do you have someone quiz you on memorized material? _____

EXERCISE B: Identifying Good Test-Taking Skills. If a statement is true, write *True* in the space provided. If it is false, write *False*.

EXAMPLE: Always do memorization work first, when you are fresh. ___*False*___

1. Cramming is exhausting, but it is the best way to prepare for a test. _____
2. To find out how well you know the material a test will cover, it helps to make up questions about it. _____
3. Reviewing notes the night before a test will only mix you up. _____
4. It is a good idea to have someone quiz you on material you are memorizing. _____
5. Memorize material by going over it repeatedly for several days before a test. _____

54.1 Using the Card Catalog

Use the card catalog to find a library book.

CATALOG CARDS

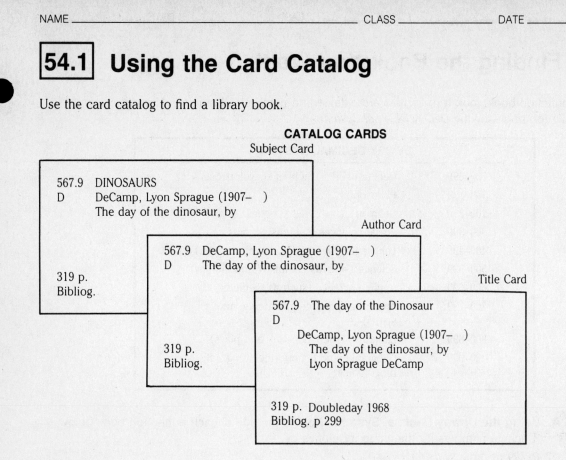

Subject Card

```
567.9   DINOSAURS
D       DeCamp, Lyon Sprague (1907–  )
        The day of the dinosaur, by



319 p.
Bibliog.
```

Author Card

```
567.9   DeCamp, Lyon Sprague (1907–  )
D          The day of the dinosaur, by



319 p.
Bibliog.
```

Title Card

```
567.9   The day of the Dinosaur
D
           DeCamp, Lyon Sprague (1907–  )
           The day of the dinosaur, by
           Lyon Sprague DeCamp



319 p. Doubleday 1968
Bibliog. p 299
```

EXERCISE A: Finding Information on Catalog Cards. Use the catalog cards above to answer the following questions.

EXAMPLE: What is the title of the book? __*The Day of the Dinosaur*__

1. Which of the three cards would come first alphabetically in the card catalog? _____

2. How many pages does this book have? _____

3. Does it have any illustrations? _____

4. What is the name of the author? _____

5. In what year was he born? _____

6. If you want to read other books by this author, what kind of card would you look for in the card catalog? _____

7. If you want to find out what other books your library has on dinosaurs, what kind of card would you look for? _____

8. On what page does the bibliography (list of books on the same subject) start? _____

9. What company published this book? _____

10. Would this book report on an attempt in 1984 to create a flying model of one kind of winged dinosaur? How can you tell? _____

EXERCISE B: Understanding Library Alphabetizing. Number the following items in the order in which they would appear in a card catalog containing all three kinds of catalog cards. One has been done for you.

1. _3_ *The Mormons and Their Religion*   2. ____ McCloskey, Robert
3. ____ Mount McKinley   4. ____ *Mary Poppins*   5. ____ *A Mountain Climber's Guide*

54.2 Finding the Book You Want

To find a nonfiction book, look it up in the card catalog and note its call number. Most libraries classify nonfiction books by the *Dewey Decimal System.*

DEWEY DECIMAL SYSTEM	
000–099	General works (such as encyclopedias)
100–199	Philosophy
200–299	Religion
300–399	Social sciences (such as economics)
400–499	Language (dictionaries, grammars, etc.)
500–599	Science (such as chemistry and biology)
600–699	Applied science (such as medicine)
700–799	Arts (music, painting, dancing, and sports)
800–899	Literature (such as poetry and plays)
900–999	Geography and history (including biographies)

EXERCISE A. Using the Dewey Decimal System. Next to the title of each nonfiction book below write the Dewey Decimal numbers for the group it belongs to.

EXAMPLE: ___700–799___ *The Skills of Soccer*

1. _____ *Robert E. Peary: North Pole Conqueror*
2. _____ *The Story of Atomic Energy*
3. _____ *Collected Poems of Emily Dickinson*
4. _____ *Cassell's French Dictionary*
5. _____ *Marie Curie: Discoverer of Radium*
6. _____ *Family Guide to Medicine*
7. _____ *The Plays of William Shakespeare*
8. _____ *The History of Ancient Rome*
9. _____ *Modern Economics*
10. _____ *The Beginner's Guide to Astronomy*

EXERCISE B: Finding Fiction. Number the following books of fiction in the order in which you would find them on the shelves of a library. The first one has been done for you.

1. _____2_____ *The Last of the Mohicans,* by James Fenimore Cooper
2. _____ *Sing Down the Moon,* by Scott O'Dell
3. _____ *Door to the North,* by Elizabeth Jane Coatsworth
4. _____ *Have Space Suit—Will Travel,* by Robert A. Heinlein
5. _____ *Mystery in Longfellow Square,* by Mary C. Jane

55.1 Using Encyclopedias

Use an encyclopedia for any of three purposes: (1) to get background information on a subject, (2) to learn basic facts about it, or (3) to find out where else to go for information.

USING AN ENCYCLOPEDIA

1. Look the subject up under its usual name. If the direction *See* . . . appears instead of an article, look up the entry suggested.
2. If the direction *See also* appears, follow up on it. An article on a related subject will often provide useful information on your topic.
3. Some articles are followed by a list of additional readings. These books or articles should be useful if you need a thorough knowledge of your topic.
4. Look your subject up in the index to the encyclopedia. Additional sources of information in the set may be found in this way.

EXERCISE A: Finding Information in Encyclopedias. Look up the following subjects. After each, write the name of the encyclopedia, the volume number, and the page on which you found information about that subject.

EXAMPLE: How paper is made _____*The New Book of Knowledge, volume 15, page 51*_____

1. Early systems of measurement _____
2. The Pony Express _____
3. The origins of baseball _____
4. How bees communicate _____
5. The origin of the Boy Scouts _____
6. The siege of Troy _____
7. The invention of the telescope _____
8. How airplanes stay up _____
9. The Magna Carta _____
10. The works of Mark Twain _____

EXERCISE B: Taking Notes in an Encyclopedia. Take brief notes on one of the topics from Exercise A or another of your choice. Give the name of the encyclopedia you use, as well as the volume and page numbers. Use another piece of paper for your answers.

EXAMPLE: How paper is made *The New Book of Knowledge,* volume 15, page 51 Wood fibers mixed with water and allowed to dry. Fibers mat together forming sheet. Sheet is dried and pressed smooth to form paper.

55.2 Using Other Reference Books

Use an almanac to get a brief answer to a question involving facts or statistics.

```
KINDS OF INFORMATION IN ALMANACS

statistics for previous year        discoverers and inventors
   (population, production           short biographies of U.S. Presidents
   in key industries,                astronomical events
   election returns)                 earthquakes and other disasters
winners of important                 postal rates and regulations
   prizes                            miscellaneous information about
sports records                          most foreign countries
```

Use an atlas for information about the geography of a region.

```
KINDS OF INFORMATION IN ATLASES

climate                    population and location of cities
natural resources             and towns
surface features of land   boundaries
                           trade routes
```

Use biographical reference books to learn important facts about a person's life.

```
SOME BIOGRAPHICAL REFERENCE BOOKS

Current Biography—short biographies of living people
Who's Who in America—facts and dates of living Americans
Who Was Who in America—facts about Americans who have
   died
Webster's Biographical Dictionary—40,000 brief biographies of
   famous people of the past and present
```

EXERCISE A: Choosing the Right Reference Book. In the space provided, write *almanac, atlas,* or *biographical reference* to indicate which reference book you would go to for information on each topic.

EXAMPLE: the discoverer of radium ___*almanac*___

1. Source of the Nile

   _____

2. First woman to win Nobel prize

   _____

3. Reason Belva Lockwood is famous

   _____

4. Capital of Oman

   _____

5. Maiden name of Nancy Reagan

   _____

6. Annual rainfall in Thailand

   _____

7. Benjamin Franklin's birthplace

   _____

8. Hurricanes of previous year

   _____

9. Mineral resources of Alaska

   _____

10. Present U.S. cabinet members

    _____

EXERCISE B: Using Other Reference Books. On a separate sheet of paper, provide the information called for in any five of the items above. Answer in complete sentences.

56.1 Finding Words Quickly

Use letter-by-letter alphabetical order to find a word in a dictionary.

KINDS OF ALPHABETICAL ORDER	
Letter-by-Letter	**Word-by-Word**
news before *New Testament*	*New Testament* before *news*
booklet before *book review*	*book review* before *booklet*
highbrow before *high jump*	*high jump* before *highbrow*
fireplace before *fire station*	*fire station* before *fireplace*

EXERCISE A: Dividing a Dictionary into Sections. Tell in which section of a dictionary each of the following words can be found:

> 1. ABCD   2. EFGHIJKL   3. MNOPQR   4. STUVWXYZ

EXAMPLE: quality __*3*__

1. hospital _____   9. demonstrate _____
2. pitiful _____   10. selfish _____
3. location _____   11. decision _____
4. ancestor _____   12. regretful _____
5. nervous _____   13. epidemic _____
6. creature _____   14. liable _____
7. sentiment _____   15. toboggan _____
8. element _____

EXERCISE B: Using Guide Words. Decide whether each word below would appear on the page with the guide words that follow it. If it would, write a + sign. If the word would come on an earlier page, write *before*. If it would come on a later page, write *after*.

EXAMPLES: quality   Quaker/quarrel __+__
             reserve   reservoir/resource __*before*__

1. run   runaway/rush _____   6. floor   flooring/flow _____
2. export   explain/express _____   7. bead   beacon/beast _____
3. nightingale nibble/nightgown _____   8. thrush thrash/throttle _____
4. chestnut   checkers/chess _____   9. dart   Darwin/daughter _____
5. stem   steep/step _____   10. poise   poison/polite _____

56.2 Understanding Main Entries

Learn to recognize and use the different kinds of information in a main entry.

SOME DIFFERENT KINDS OF MAIN-ENTRY INFORMATION

1. How a word is spelled
2. Syllabification—how a word is divided into syllables
3. Pronunciation
4. The part, or parts, of speech of a word
5. Etymology—the origin and history of a word
6. Definition—the different meanings a word can have

EXERCISE A: Using a Dictionary for Syllable Division. Look up the following words. Write each one with a slanting line at each place where the word can be broken into syllables. Circle the syllable that is most heavily stressed.

EXAMPLE: revolution ___*rev/o/(lu)tion*___

1. latitude _____

2. habitat _____

3. Fahrenheit _____

4. punctuation _____

5. suspicious _____

6. appreciation _____

7. Tallahassee _____

8. literature _____

9. athletic _____

10. chocolate _____

EXERCISE B: Finding Other Information in Main Entries. Use your dictionary to answer each question below.

EXAMPLE: The part of speech of *slowly* ___*adv.*___

1. the word used in the pronunciation key to show the sound of the vowel in the word *shrewd*.

_____

2. the etymology (origin and history) of *rival* _____

3. the number of numbered definitions for *plum* _____

4. another spelling for tennis *racket* _____

5. the plural of *mongoose* _____

NAME _____ CLASS _____ DATE _____

57.1 Preparing Yourself to Listen Well

Get physically and mentally ready to listen.

MENTAL PREPARATION FOR LISTENING

1. *Do* tell yourself: "I will listen and pay attention."
2. *Do* focus your eyes and ears on the speaker.
3. *Do* put away things that can distract you.
4. *Do* take notes in class.
5. *Do* block out other concerns and thoughts.
6. *Don't* daydream.
7. *Don't* look around at your friends in class.
8. *Don't* doodle.
9. *Don't* stop listening to speakers just because their opinions are different from your own.
10. *Don't* ignore speakers just because they are saying things you already know.

EXERCISE A: Evaluating Your Listening Skills. Rate yourself on how well you listened during a recent class, auditorium program, or other listening opportunity. Answer each question *Yes* or *No*.

EXAMPLE: Did you doodle? __*No*__

1. Did you remind yourself to pay attention at the start? _____

2. Did you keep your eyes on the speaker? _____

3. Did your posture show your interest? _____

4. Did you try to block out other thoughts and concerns? _____

5. Did you doodle? _____

6. Did you take notes? _____

7. Did you whisper or look around at friends? _____

8. Did you daydream? _____

9. Did you stop listening if you thought you knew what the speaker was going to say? _____

10. Did you stop listening if the speaker said something you didn't agree with? _____

EXERCISE B: Improving Your Listening Skills. Watch an informational program on television and rate your listening performance, using the questions in Exercise A once more. Pay special attention to points you were weak on in Exercise A.

57.2 Listening for Main Ideas

Be alert for main ideas as you listen.

HOW TO SPOT MAIN IDEAS

1. Listen for ideas mentioned at the beginning of a class, lecture or other speaking occasion.
2. Listen for ideas mentioned at the end.
3. Notice which ideas are repeated.
4. Be alert for spoken clues; for example, "Remember . . . ," "Most important . . . ," "First of all . . . ," "To summarize . . . ."
5. Notice what is written on the blackboard.
6. Notice when the speaker's voice becomes louder, or more emphatic.
7. Ask yourself more than once, "What is the main point of what I am hearing? What ties everything together?"
8. If necessary, ask the speaker to make clear what the main point is.

EXERCISE A: Spotting Main Ideas. Watch an informational program on television (or listen to one on radio). Using the suggestions on the chart, pick out the main ideas of the lecture or program. Then answer the questions below.

1. The main idea(s) of the lecture or program was (were) _____

2. Were the main ideas stated at the start? _____

3. Were the main points reviewed at the end? _____

4. Were any ideas repeated during the presentation? _____

5. Were spoken clues (*remember, most important, to summarize*) used to help you spot important ideas? _____

6. Did the speaker's voice suggest which ideas were especially important? _____

7. Were transitional words like *so, therefore,* and *furthermore* used to help you follow the train of thought? _____

8. Were visual devices used to highlight important ideas? _____

9. Which parts of the program were used to illustrate main ideas? _____

_____

10. If you had had the opportunity, what question(s) would you have asked the speaker or presenter?

_____

_____

EXERCISE B. Improving Your Listening Skills. On a separate sheet of paper, write a paragraph describing the listening skill(s) you most need to improve and how you intend to go about doing so.

58.1 Participating in Class

Participate actively in your classes.

HOW TO PARTICIPATE IN CLASS

1. Do whatever studying and homework is required of you so that you come to class prepared to participate.
2. Listen attentively.
3. To conquer shyness, keep your mind on the class.
4. Ask questions when you are unclear about something—it is likely that other students are unclear about it too.
5. Ask questions to follow up something said in a discussion.
6. When your teacher asks a question of the class that you can answer, raise your hand and, if called on, give your answer.
7. Do not interrupt other speakers or call out answers.

EXERCISE A: Evaluating Your Class Participation. Answer the following questions as honestly as you can. Use only the first blank for Exercise A.

EXAMPLE: Do I listen attentively to the teacher? _____Yes_____ _____

1. Do I complete homework so that I can take part in classroom discussions? _____ _____

2. Do I enjoy taking part in class discussions? _____ _____

3. Am I reluctant to answer a question because it might be the wrong answer? _____ _____

4. Do I pay attention to the answers of my classmates? _____ _____

5. Do I ask questions when something is not clear? _____ _____

6. Do I hesitate to ask questions for fear of sounding foolish? _____ _____

7. Do I follow up the answers or comments of others with my own comments? _____ _____

8. Do I ever daydream during class discussions? _____ _____

9. Do I volunteer answers to my teacher's questions? _____ _____

10. Do I let others speak without interrupting them? _____ _____

EXERCISE B. Improving Your Listening Skills. Study your weak points in class participation as revealed in Exercise A. After one week, use these questions to reevaluate yourself. This time, use the right-hand set of blanks.

58.2 Preparing a Short Speech

Prepare for a speech by collecting and organizing your thoughts on your topic and by practicing your delivery.

GETTING READY FOR A SPEECH

1. Build your speech on a single-sentence statement of one main idea.
2. Make sure any reasons or explanations you use are clear and easy to follow.
3. Use simple, vivid examples and illustrations to clarify your reasons or explanations.
4. Plan to open your speech with an attention-getting statement.
5. Plan to conclude your speech with a vivid, memorable restatement of your main idea.
6. Jot your main idea and supporting statements on index cards you can glance at while speaking.
7. Above all, avoid reading at your listeners: Look at them and speak slowly and clearly. Rely on your memory and, when necessary, a quick glance at your cards.

EXERCISE A: Making Notes for a Speech. Select a topic from the list below or another you think of yourself. Narrow it to make a specific subject for a short speech. Then follow the numbered directions.

Care of a Pet   Practical Jokes
Television Commercials   An Unforgettable Experience
A Needed School Improvement   My Favorite Sport

EXAMPLE: A Needed School Improvement
              We need longer lunch periods.

1. Make notes on 3×5 cards.
2. State your main idea in one sentence.
3. If you are trying to persuade, write each reason you will use on a separate card.
4. If you are trying to explain, list each example or illustration on its own card.
5. If you are telling a story, write a brief phrase to remind you of incidents you will use.
6. Write a word or phrase on your last card to remind you of your concluding statement.

EXERCISE B. Practicing Your Speech. First review your note cards, planning what you will say about each point. Then rehearse your speech, glancing at the cards only when you need to.